Blueprint FOR THE Contact Center OF THE Future

Blueprint *FOR THE* Contact Center *OF THE* Future

The IT guide for relevancy, resources, and results.

Erin Wilson

Director at Five9

Erin Wilson

A charismatic engineer, Erin cleverly pairs technical expertise with business acumen to communicate complex concepts to technical and non-technical audiences alike. A 15-year SaaS veteran, Erin challenges companies to creatively apply contact center technology to their most strategic initiatives, and helps organizations deliver exceptional, engaging customer experiences. She is an author and frequently guides thought leadership discussions on technology. Erin has held senior and leadership positions in Technical Marketing, Solutions Consulting, Product Evangelism, and Business Partner Enablement.

Published with the support of Five9 by Erin Wilson
Hollywood, FL

Authored by: Erin Wilson
Edited by: Kim Austin
Illustrations and cover art by: Arthur Waidhofer
Forward by: Maribel Lopez

ISBN. 978-0-9962373-1-4

To all my IT friends who are tired of being seen as obstacles
when only trying to help.

AN INDUSTRY PERSPECTIVE

In today's digital age, customer experience (CX) is a top priority for businesses of all sizes, but getting it right can often feel like an elusive goal. Part of the challenge is that in order to crack the code of great CX externally, the barriers we often put up internally within the business need to be broken down. Great CX is about leveraging technology and people to deliver a great employee experience as well as customer experience. Great CX requires collaboration.

In *Blueprint for the Contact Center of the Future*, Erin Wilson brings to bear her 18+ years of experience working with brands to understand and deploy technology to help buyers navigate the nuanced dance that teams must perform to, together, find success. Starting with the role and relationship between IT and the contact center, she provides the reader with practical advice from how to build a business case, to how to ensure you are AI ready. With the objective of delivering a recipe for success, *Blueprint for the Contact Center of the Future* shows how fostering the intelligent collaboration between people and technology, and between customer and employee, has the potential to shepherd in a new age for the contact center and those who support it.

Genefa Murphy
PhD User Acceptance of New Technology and CMO of Five9

FOREWORD

Today, the contact center serves more than a support function. It's the face of the brand's customer experience. In a world of distributed, hybrid work organizations, companies need a playbook that helps them to deliver a holistic strategy that spans infrastructure, software, and processes. Wilson's book provides guidelines for how to design the foundation of this experience, covering every aspect from building facilities to dealing with technical debt and designing the future of employee experiences.

Maribel Lopez
Industry Analyst, Author, Technology Influencer

TABLE OF CONTENTS

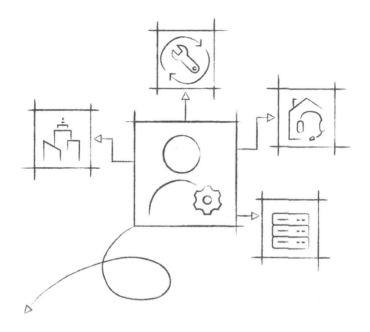

INTRODUCTION

Just when you think you have a handle on the pace of change, the universe throws a wrench in the works. Having spent my whole career in cloud technologies, I came to enjoy the slow-but-steady pace at which clients adopted the various tools I represented. And then boom! 2020 drops the pandemic bomb and sends us all home.

The world, not just the contact center, has changed. Whether on Zoom, Netflix, or Instacart, many of us — even our most technophobic relatives — landed in the cloud. With employees no longer physically near the on-premises equipment they depended on, the contact center space — my longstanding professional home — saw rapid acceleration replace the steady pace of change. The need for change spanned all aspects of the contact center space, from infrastructure and operations to changes in customer and employee expectations — and even where people work.

All this change drives the need for IT and business units to find more common ground and ways to collaborate to drive business agility.

My goal is to offer IT professionals the insights you need to influence change at the executive level. I'll provide perspective on the contact center of the future, plus a practical approach to selecting the tools and technologies to affect strategic change within your organization. Along the way we'll introduce you to some characters who have experienced these adventures in their own organizations and have wisdom — and warnings — to share. Some suggestions may seem like common sense, others may seem random, but they're all designed to provoke thought and — most important — inspire action.

Recent History of the Contact Center

First, a little history. It's a funny thing: The first call center agents in the 1950s were remote workers. Specifically, women working from home using phone directories to sell baked goods and Tupperware. It only took a pandemic to bring many organizations back to the industry's roots, back to the realization that choice and hybrid work environments can be empowering for the individual and the business.

As telephony technology evolved over the decades, so did the industry and prevalence of telemarketing. Call centers existed as largely outbound sales channels until the 1980s with the mass adoption of toll-free numbers. Finally, companies realized the best way to encourage customers to call them was to relieve them of the long-distance charges. Customers could easily use a central number to respond to marketing efforts or ask for support — for free.

With a mix of inbound and outbound calls, agent roles evolved as well. Outbound agents addressed sales activities, while inbound agents focused more on support and customer satisfaction. And routing the calls through that central number introduced the need for more integrated systems so agents could just as easily help Kyle in Kalamazoo as Frank in Fresno.

The next major evolution landed in your inbox. Consumer internet access spiked the adoption of email in the 1990s, making it a primary way to reach out to companies, whether for business or personal needs. Although it would take a couple dozen years to complete, this began the shift from call centers toward multichannel contact centers.

As website capabilities matured, they gave rise to online businesses — especially in retail. With more online-only operations in the dot-com boom, contact centers took more direct responsibility to address the needs of customers. For many companies, that meant there was no longer a service desk hidden at the back of the store where employees handled customer issues in person. Now, if your vacuum cleaner broke, you'd pick up the phone or go online instead of hauling it down to the shop.

Telephony advancements also helped businesses centralize their call centers into fewer locations where agents could have access to complex customer information systems — and managers could easily track their work. Many organizations looked to offshore alternatives to reduce costs by engaging with companies in areas with a lower cost of living.

Each evolution of technology brought new opportunities — and new challenges — to contact centers. From corded phones at the kitchen table to online dashboards managing multiple communications channels, customer access to technology continues to drive the need for innovation. As customer expectations evolve, so must those of us responsible for the contact center.

Fast forward to today: Customers expect swift response to and resolution of their needs, whether by phone, email, web chat, messaging, or self-service options. Live agents remain a critical part of the equation even as artificial intelligence, virtual agents, and automation become a bigger part of the mix. As these new technologies increase in prevalence, the skills required to design, build, and maintain the contact center will evolve.

CHAPTER ONE

A New Path for IT Professionals

The IT role has already changed a dozen times. Ask anyone who started their IT journey 30 years — heck, 15 years — ago. You'll hear stories of some technology or another that surely stood to disrupt or replace their roles. Honestly, how many "digital transformations" have we done in the past 30 years?! When the dust settles, the addition of this technology typically results in more interesting, if not more vital, roles for IT.

No one ever needs less IT.

IT Roles Will Change

When I first exited school with a degree in applied math, the job market wasn't great; I was happy to take whatever job I could get. Shortly thereafter I thought "if this is what a bachelor's degree gets you, I need a master's!" So, I went back to school part time and pursued a degree in computer science. Unfortunately, the lesson with the most impact was how much writing code made me want to put out my eye. I'm an idea-haver, not a debug queen. Once I solved the puzzle, the code should work, the fun was over, and I lacked the patience or desire to see it through. So, I got a job doing tech support — lots of puzzles, all day long.

I enjoyed it, but customers — especially new ones — kept coming to us with really silly questions. They wanted the application to do things it didn't actually do. Naturally, I blamed sales. Clearly, they were lying. So, I put on my 20-something hero-complex cape and decided I would go into sales engineering and prevent such misconceptions before they even had a chance to sprout.

I learned another important lesson. It turns out letting the customer believe a little fairy tale is fundamental to the sales engineering profession. But I took my role of "technical conscience" in the deal seriously. And I loved the job; more puzzles, even less follow through.

Now, as a leader inside a software company's marketing organization, I enjoy a new perspective and a more novel set of customer challenges to solve. I love it. But I can't help but chuckle when I think about how I got here. How did a math major go from doing tech support to hosting sales methodology workshops overseas to writing marketing material? It comes down to one thing: I never lost my willingness to go with the flow and approach challenges as opportunities.

Perhaps your career has taken a similar, wandering, path. Whether you knew IT was your calling from the onset, you found it along the way, or it's a mere stop along your path toward finding your passion, you can appreciate the need for adaptability.

The person you were 20 years ago isn't the same person you see in the mirror today.

Especially with respect to the contact center, IT's role will change. The value you and your organization can offer a contact center will extend beyond cabling and vector programming. If you're ready, it's time to break out of the IT closet and explore opportunities to add tremendous, strategic value to your organization — even more than you do today — while learning new things and challenging the status quo. It all starts with your willingness to embrace the change that's already happening around you.

Define Your New Role

As with the digital transformations that have come before it, the transformation from call center to contact center brings opportunity. An opportunity to carve your own path. To learn new skills. To explore emerging technology. To become the kind of change agent you imagined when first considering a career in IT.

Increasingly, contact centers will need forward-thinkers who can see the big picture while still catching all the details that IT business partners seem to miss. We no longer have to fit into one of the four, stereotypical IT Pro boxes: telephony people, network people, software people, or internal IT people. This is a chance to break free and ask yourself: What aspects of the latest digital transformation trend or next-generation technology platforms pique your interest? Will you become an artificial intelligence (AI) specialist? Will you master machine learning? Does process automation make your heart go pitter patter? Or are you like me — more thinker than doer, who loves coming up with creative ideas and inspiring people around me to bring them to life?

The role of IT in the contact center of the future will be a consulting one. One that requires expert-level big-picture mindfulness. One in which technical zeal fuels strategic ideas. One that inspires the business leaders that you support to try new things and adopt the latest technology.

With the rise of software-as-a-service (SaaS) applications, the mechanics of managing business software shifts to the laps of the individual line of business owners, leaving your team some (hopefully) much-appreciated space to advise more, (physically) do less, and track project results more than the minutia.

How Much Decision Power *Should* IT Have?

As an ex-sales engineer, I have to say that having IT folks in a deal used to scare me. Y'all would always come armed with so many detailed questions. And while I (usually) knew the answers, the interrogations could get intense. In the end, since the answers were good — if I do say so myself — my new IT friends would relent and allow the meeting, usually arranged by the business decision maker, to continue. But what struck me wasn't the line of questioning. Their hearts were in the right place. But it was the looks on faces of the business leaders — and for that matter, the salespeople — while it was happening.

They looked at IT like someone was kicking a puppy. Here they were, waist deep in the decision, when IT came along with a bucket of questions they didn't understand. All they heard was doubt because many of them didn't understand all the questions. It felt like the whole room let out a collective sigh when an IT representative reached for their proverbial rubber stamp and allowed the deal to continue.

One business leader pulled me aside after a meeting. "I'm sorry, the IT department is always that last group of hurdles in a track race," he said. "You need to jump over them to get to the finish line." That's not a great way to be perceived!

If you're in IT, how much is too much power for you to have in the decision-making process for new tech? Should IT have veto power? Should IT own the initial requirements gathering? Or should you hand the whole project over to the business units with a bow and say "Good luck chumps"?

When you can't see the forest for the trees it's probably a good time to relinquish control. But how much control you let go will depend on a few factors.

- Who will own the maintenance and administration?
- Who will oversee the implementation?
- How much integration work is necessary?

And so on. Just remember you also don't want to get stuck trying to force the business units to buy into what IT chose. By then it's too late to achieve the kind of consensus that breeds successful projects and strong adoption.

Part of the goal of this book it to help you find the "happy medium" for your business. My primary advice at this point: No single person should hold all the power.

We've seen how that plays out in world politics, let alone in the office. Respect that your business users know what they are trying to accomplish better than you do. And try to respect a vendor that fights you on the "how to do it." Sometimes they have a perspective worth considering. Be pragmatic and open. We're all trying to get to the same place: the contact center of the future.

Building the Contact Center of the Future

Now that we understand the new role supporting the contact center, let's look at how to choose a solution that supports the type of forward-thinking, strategic-influencer role IT deserves.

Because no one wants to shop for major technology solutions over and over, this book will help you evaluate and choose a "forever home" for your contact center. And — as promised — we'll point out opportunities for you to stand out as a thought leader within your organization.

So, let's get building!

Albert: A 40-year Perspective

Albert is an IT practitioner who has worked for a popular public university for four decades. Having started as an intern, he now heads the IT department and will be remembered for his role in completely transforming the university's contact center. He acknowledges that many of his accomplishments would have been impossible without a radical change in his mindset and having a team of high-value strategic thinkers surrounding him.

Albert: Forty years! That's how long I've worked here. And yet it still feels like yesterday — everywhere but my knees. I started as an intern just a few days after graduating from the same university. Everything started with the administration's vote of confidence that I've been gladly repaying for the last four decades.

Indeed, time flies when you love what you are doing.

Now, as I near my retirement, I can't help but reminisce on how things have changed since my days as an intern. I've loved watching the contact center evolve into the current modern setup that can handle more than 70,000 inbound and outbound calls per week.

I've worked with all the university's departments, but the contact center is my passion project. It's probably because of how critical it has been in driving growth. It hasn't been without sacrifices though. When the university introduced online courses in 2000, the unprecedented surge in traffic from interested students and parents had us working around the clock for months to keep up.

When I first started working here, the call center was based on a PBX phone system. For the uninitiated, PBX stands for private branch exchange; it's a traditional phone system that relied on physical handsets and telephone cables. Automatic call routing didn't exist yet, so we relied on human switchboard operators to connect callers to the right agents.

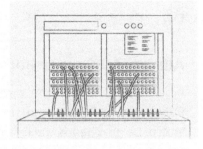

Fortunately, this did not have to go on for too long due to the emergence of Private Automatic Branch Exchanges (PABX) in the late 1970s. We didn't get ours until the early 1980s when I spearheaded the PABX implementation. It was my first major project. The instant effect it had on both employee attitude and business operations have driven me to invest so much time and effort in transforming the contact center.

The new PABX allowed us to create a recorded message to greet all our customers. And because it also supported voice over internet protocol (VoIP) calls, it led to a dramatic increase in call volume. Luckily, we handled the spike by training the now-obsolete switchboard operators to become call agents. If you had asked me then, I would have sworn that there couldn't be a better system.

Imagine my shock and delight when I first encountered contact center software. A solution that not only enhanced the calling experience but introduced other communication options including email, web chat, and social media messaging? Win. It also meant we could integrate with our customer relationship management (CRM) software, allowing us to offer personalized support since agents now had access to important customer information.

Ironically, the colleague who introduced me to the solution didn't come from a technical background. Meghan was a marketing major and possessed a deep understanding of how businesses could leverage software to improve both customer and workforce experience.

I had focused on keeping our current systems up and running, thinking it was necessary to keep the institution thriving. In doing so, I forgot the importance of continuous innovation. At this point, I also lead recruiting for the IT department. Meghan helped me realize that I had been putting so much emphasis on candidates' technical skills that I neglected core soft skills like creativity, resourcefulness, communication, problem-solving, and adaptability.

The result? A pool of individuals who thrived only under orders. It shouldn't come as a surprise, therefore, that I recruited Meghan into my team. One of the best decisions I've made in my career.

When 2020 came and many businesses were closing everywhere due to the pandemic, it was the opposite for us. With people confined to their homes, demand for online courses surged and students flooded our call center. Our agents could no longer field all the incoming calls as well as make necessary outbound calls.

We had been discussing the need to move our systems to the cloud, but Covid-19 was the motivation we needed to make the move. We decided we would start with our contact center software. Again, Meghan came through in a major way when I tasked her with finding the perfect solution for us.

It's almost two years since we moved to CCaaS. Our contact center has completely transformed. One of the main benefits is we've been able to add more agents without having to expand our current facility. We have more than 200 remote agents all over the world. And thanks to smart call routing, we connect incoming callers with the most competent agent.

We also don't have to worry about traffic surges since the cloud solution allows us to scale easily as we need to. Additionally, functions such as interactive voice response (IVR[1]) and intelligent virtual agents (IVAs) are even more efficient thanks to AI.

And as I look back at my career, I can't help but imagine how much things could have been different. Without that one moment that led me to shift my mindset, I would have probably stuck to my old ways. University growth would likely have stagnated, and I would have, most definitely, been replaced with someone more idealistic.

Having given my everything to my job only to receive nothing in the end, it would have all circled back to that one moment: And I would be a very miserable old man.

---

[1] Interactive voice response systems are those old-school, press 1 for this,2 for that, phone systems popularized in the 1990s.

CHAPTER TWO

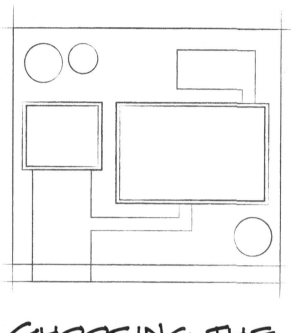

CHOOSING THE PERFECT PLOT OF LAND

Where you build your forever home is as important as what it looks like. Just as climate change might influence your plot selection for your actual home, you must decide whether to set up business on-premises, in the cloud, or somewhere in between.

Cloud vs. On-Premises Solutions

The differences between cloud and on-premises solutions are as philosophical as they are tangible. Tradeoffs exist with either choice. To effectively decide between the two, you first must decide by which yardsticks you plan to measure the solutions.

By Total Cost of Ownership

While both on-premises and cloud solutions come with one-time and recurring costs, the ratios of those numbers often vary wildly. To evaluate the total cost of ownership, first choose a time window. Given the speed of customer and market changes, we recommend three to five years[2]. For budgetary purposes, cloud solutions typically find their funding in operating budgets. On-premises solutions, due to heavy up-front hardware costs, are generally a capital expense — but that's not the whole story.

Apples to Apples

Many technologists fall victim to the allure of the apples-to-apples comparison. And who can blame them? It feels so scientific: You get to use spreadsheets, identify all the variables, and then it's just math. Simple, right? Well, if your otherwise attractive spread-sheet is missing rows, the math simply won't add up. To make matters worse, not every cost from on-prem will apply to cloud (see figure 2-1 on opposite page).

    The economics of cloud and on-premises solutions are very different. Attempting to compare their true total cost of ownership will quickly begin to look more like calculus than arithmetic. I don't want to bury you in math, so instead, here's a checklist of the sometimes-overlooked costs associated with the two solution types.

Supporting Remote Workers

I started working from home in 2005 when I got a tech support job off Craigslist with a private CRM company. I remember calling my dad to see if he could confirm that "SugarCRM" was a real company before I put in notice at my old gig. The deal seemed too good to be true: 25% more money and 100% work from home?!? And they didn't even want to fly me out for an interview.

---

[2] Pay special attention to year four when many on-premises vendors impose changes to their hardware maintenance requirements as they can significantly change the TCO calculus.

Costs to Consider	On-Prem	Cloud
Hardware		
Hardware to run the solution	$$$	n/a
Power and HVAC	$	n/a
Home for the hardware (on- or off-site data center)	$$	n/a
Maintenance	$$	n/a
Software		
Annualized cost	$	$
Support	Not included	Included
Maintenance	Not included	Included
Implementation		
Professional Services	$$	$
Training	$	Typically included
Upgrades	$	Included
Expansions	$	$
Incremental costs of adding users	$$$	$
Shrinkage	Costs remain	Costs reduce
Staff required to support	$$$	$

Figure 2-1: Apples to oranges costs comparison of on-premises and cloud solutions

(This was before the ubiquity of Zoom.) I had three or four phone interviews and then boom: job offer. It was almost too easy. Sugar is in fact a real company and proved to be a great way to spend the next five years.

Today remote work and interviewing aren't only common, they're the cost of doing business for many industries. To attract and recruit the best talent, you need to make all the flexibility of workplace options available to candidates. The ability to work from home has become a critical component of a contact center forever home.

When considering a solution's total cost of ownership, you must consider the cost of the "unexpected." The pandemic served as an unwelcome wake-up call for many organizations when they were forced to relocate their office workers to work-from-home setups. For those utilizing on-premises contact center solutions, this proved to be costly and cumbersome. But the sudden and urgent need to pick up and move isn't limited to a (hopefully) once-in-a-lifetime occurrence like a pandemic.

Severe weather, sudden unforeseen demand, power outages, fire, or just overall employee needs for more flexibility are all reasons your contact center might need to relocate in a hurry. Whether you send your staff home, relocate to a temporary location, or stand up new offices frequently, consider the costs of doing so:

- Do you have to buy more equipment?
- What about connectivity?
- Is there budget to provide work-from-home employees a monthly internet stipend?

The Costs of Downtime

What happens when your system becomes inaccessible? Over 70% of my customers consider their contact centers a revenue driver (as opposed to simply a cost center). If that ratio extends to the greater market (and my research suggests it does), the business risks of downtime have never been higher. To evaluate this, final, component of the total cost of ownership, you need to identify how much revenue your contact center business both brings in per hour — typical of sales centers — and how much the business stands to lose in customer attrition if they suddenly aren't reachable.

The first of the two calculations is much easier to obtain, so start there. Don't forget about upsells. Some customer support or service contact centers — like insurance, mortgage, even scheduling — make a point of sharing new promotions with their customers. For example: You call an airline to change your flight and end up also making a car rental reservation. These more subtle sales and referral practices can generate considerable revenue, so consider their value in your total cost of ownership calculation.

It's harder to measure the correlation between downtime and attrition. Don't fret: Your line-of-business counterparts watch several leading indicators — like customer satisfaction (CSAT) — to estimate a customer's likelihood of jumping to another vendor. Combine their metrics with data from before and after your last outage or temporary closure to get a good proxy for the value of the book of business you're "insuring" by choosing a contact center solution that's both reliable and nimble. While this argument may seem too far outside the scope of IT's purview to bother with, it's a statistic that C-level executives are concerned with as it's a leading indicator of revenue. The more you can align yourself with big-picture cost savings, the more likely you'll garner the support you need to fund your initiatives.

Uptime

Everyone involved in a high-dollar, visible solution purchase lends a little of their personal reputation to the selection. So, it's natural to compare the uptime and expected reliability of possible solutions. The telecom world measures expected system availability as a percentage of 100. Historically, "five nines" or 99.999% uptime was the gold standard. If your system could achieve that, you can consider yourself proud.

No solution will have 100% uptime.

To calculate the amount of downtime you can expect from different solutions, multiply the number of minutes in a year (381,600) by 1 minus the estimated uptime (1 - 0.99999 = 0.00001). Figure 2-2 shows the expected annual downtime for systems achieving varying amounts of uptime.

	2 nines 99.0% uptime	3 nines 99.9% uptime	4 nines 99.99% uptime	5 nines 99.999% uptime	6 nines 99.9999% uptime
Annual Down-time	3,816 minutes	381.6 minutes	38.16 minutes	3.82 minutes	0.38 minutes
	2.65 days	6.36 hours			< 23 seconds

Figure 2-2: Translating Downtime Percentages to Minutes

Set your expectations to match your business objectives. And remember: The expected system availability for on-premises solutions is defined by the availability of the weakest solution or solution component. Any single point of failure will potentially bring it down, no matter how much hardening you do to the rest of the system.

To achieve expected uptime nearing 99.999%, you may need to add — and budget for — additional hardware, facilities, circuits, and more to achieve the redundancy necessary for the resiliency you desire.

Spoiler alert: Cloud solutions provide the economies of scale that come when you can share hardware costs and other infrastructure investments with other organizations. Consequently, cloud solutions typically offer superior uptime at a fraction of the cost of on-premises applications. And as an added benefit of cloud, all the headaches of uptime and downtime are someone else's problem.

Business Agility

There's a real estate saying: "You can change everything else, but you can't change your view." It speaks to our tendency to invest in our homes only to realize that it was really the location that disappoints. Luckily for a homeowner, the cost of a new kitchen will theoretically increase the home's value to a potential buyer.

Unfortunately, businesses don't typically have a mechanism to recoup all the time, effort, and cash they invest in a project if (and when) they realize it's time for a change. That's why business agility is such a hot topic.

How can you choose (create) an environment for your future contact center that will adapt the "view" to your future business needs without devaluing the investments you've made thus far?

IT professionals with previous experience with on-premises solutions can appreciate the instinct to double down. It's like a homeowner who contends that a flooding basement isn't a reason to move simply because they just redid the bathroom and feel like they need to "get the return" from that effort. A business that just spent big bucks on an upgrade might feel obligated to depreciate the investment before moving on. Or worse, they might "water-proof" the basement instead of admitting they live in a flood plain.

If this sounds familiar, if you feel stuck, or you don't want to admit defeat — because doing so would negatively impact your reputation or bottom line — remember that it usually costs more (much more), to stay in a bad situation longer than necessary.

To be better, you must first be different. The more quickly you can accept the need for change, the sooner you can realize the results of those changes and put the technical debt behind you, once and for all.

Cloud providers uniquely offer business agility — in every sense of the word.

Location, Location, Location

By removing the physical location requirement of agents, cloud consumers aren't encumbered by the natural disasters, local connectivity challenges, and office closures that can plague their on-premises brethren. Sure, all those things can still happen, but the cloud offers greater agility to shrug off location-related challenges. Your users can access cloud solutions from nearly anywhere, telephony and connectivity are typically handled in-region, and midweek relocations — whatever the impetus — are a non-event: Users simply log in from wherever they are and away they go.

Freedom from Upgrades

The cloud provides automatic access to the latest solution or technology. Cloud vendors, like Google, deliver new capabilities to users all the time. Your Gmail account looks nothing like it did 15 years ago. But can you even remember it changing? Magically, the UI remains fresh and modern. And new, updated capabilities — think integration with Google Calendar or Google Meet — were added without you giving it a second thought.

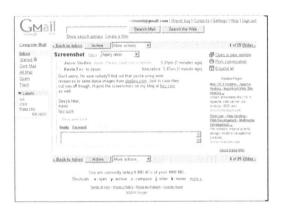

Figure 2-3. Screenshot of Gmail webmail interface in 2004.[3]

Figure 2-4. Screenshot of Gmail webmail interface in 2022.

---

[3] Jason Shellen, "1GB of email — you're kidding right?" Shellen.com, April 2004, https://www.shellen.com/1gb-of-email-you-kidding-right

That's the advantage of choosing a good cloud vendor: You get new things (features) before you even ask.

In the contact center space, your expectations should be even higher! Choose a vendor with a great product vision, clearly defined roadmap, and a history of delivering capabilities that clients needed even before the market demanded them. By receiving automatic upgrades, you'll always have the solutions you need to address customer demand — when you need them. No more planning expensive upgrades or migrations. Just continuous, incremental improvement that adapts and anticipates the needs of the market.

As a bonus, consider a vendor that has an active user community or customer advisory board. This demonstrates their willingness to listen to customer feedback in addition to market drivers and provides you with an opportunity to influence the changes you wish to see in the technology as it evolves.

The best part of this kind of cloud-powered agility is that it also keeps you nimble. Business leaders who choose agile solutions get to expand their personal knowledge and skill set over time. This helps you future-proof your own career path, and it's much less daunting than learning a whole new technology from scratch. Don't worry. Just like how Google works hard to make Gmail super intuitive, leading cloud contact center providers have invested heavily in usability research. Expect more clicks-not-code user experiences and powerful, yet intuitive, development environments — even when it comes to things like training AI engines.

Subscription Businesses Need You to Succeed

Unlike solutions that require a rich, upfront capital investment, a cloud provider's revenue streams depend on retaining you as a customer. They have financial incentive to ensure you succeed; partner with a vendor as invested in your success as you are.

If you're not on team cloud yet, please fight the instinct to research cloud simply to arm yourself with the ammunition to shoot down cloud proposals. A desire to know thy enemy might initiate your research, but realize: Cloud is often the best decision for the business.

Consider a move to the cloud as an opportunity for you to learn and grow personally while adding differentiated value to your team and company. Lean on your solution partners to get the training you need to ensure success. It takes more than technology to achieve true business agility: We must also change our minds.

> IT TAKES MORE THAN TECHNOLOGY TO ACHIEVE TRUE BUSINESS AGILITY: WE MUST ALSO CHANGE OUR MINDS.

Relinquishing Control

Is your IT department a team of helicopter moms? Can you blame them? After years of watching users make terrifying decisions with personal devices, naïve tech vendor choices, and embarrassing implementation selections, it's natural to want to provide some "adult supervision."

When noodling a move to the cloud, it's understandable to hesitate at the idea of relinquishing control of the devices, servers, and technologies that run your business — especially with something as high stakes as the contact center. You're in good company — both in your hesitation and your path.

Many, many companies have come before you. Even companies in highly regulated environments like financial services and healthcare feel confident in moving to the cloud or using hosted data centers. The key difference to consider, then, becomes:

What's riskier — putting all my eggs in one, personal, basket that I control myself or spreading the risk across the several locations, data centers, and the baked-in resiliency that cloud solutions can provide?

When you dig into the architecture, the best solution for you will become very clear. Trust, verify, and delegate responsibility.

Hybrid Prem + Cloud Solutions

Hybrid solutions can be appealing. They seem to offer a chance to dip your toe into something new. In reality, they're the worst of both worlds.

Not only must you still manage, maintain, and monitor all the on-premises stuff, you have to build a bridge between the two application environments. That's another MPLS (multiprotocol label switching[4]) line, another point of failure, and more to worry about. Hiring for hybrid can mean needing twice the expertise. Will all that knowledge reside in the same person? Or will you need more staff to manage something that's supposed to simplify things?

The only circumstance where I'd recommend a hybrid solution is when you're so recently and deeply invested in your on-premises application that it's financially unfeasible to walk away in the near term. Rather than allow your competition to benefit from the technology advancements the cloud offers while your company depreciates its dinosaur, consider layering a cloud solution on top. It can enhance the customer experience and help keep you competitive in the meantime.

But generally speaking: If you're going to pay for cloud, get cloud.

---

[4] Essentially, it's a dedicated private "internet" circuit between the systems it connects. Companies buy MPLS circuits for performance and security reasons.

If Cloud, Which Cloud?

Cloud contact center vendors, commonly known as contact center as a service (CCaaS) providers, still have to host their solutions somewhere. They, too, must pick a cloud. The choices they make — opting for public, private, or hybrid cloud — affect the overall reliability and scalability of their solutions, which impact you.

Let's discuss the merits and risks of each so you can decide for yourself which model best aligns with your business strategy and priorities.

Public Cloud

Public cloud is a computing model that offers resources via a remote internet connection and charges on a pay-per-use pricing model. It's best suited for very large software development or collaboration projects and offers a high level of reliability and uptime, making it a common choice for CCaaS vendors. Popular public cloud providers include Amazon Web Services (AWS), Google Cloud Platform (GCP), and Microsoft Azure.

Vendors choose to host their solutions via public cloud because, at scale, they quickly deliver large ROI thanks to the ability to scale at a nearly infinite measure and speed. Public clouds protect the vendor from the same type of capital expenditures and maintenance costs that you're seeking to avoid by moving to the cloud.

There are downsides to a vendor deploying entirely on public cloud, however, including margin compression and loss of control over the service and uptime of the hosting provider. Consequently, as CCaaS providers grow, you may see them begin to adopt a more balanced approach, splitting their costs and risks over multiple public-cloud providers or adopting a hybrid of public- and private-cloud strategies.

Private Clouds

A private cloud is also accessed by end users via an internet connection. Unlike a public cloud where multiple organizations might share access to a single physical box, private clouds are segmented.

Only one business entity uses the allocated resources. The old client-server models were essentially private clouds: A business would own the server space and its consumers would privately access its content from remote locations.

Today, some CCaaS providers choose private clouds for the control and security they offer the company. You can host these private clouds in your own data centers, but they're more commonly hosted by a third-party provider such as Equinix or CoreSite. This model is best suited for organizations that require a high degree of customization or security beyond what public-cloud vendors provide.

Government agencies and financial institutions are the most common users of private clouds, so you'll see this option more often in the tech stacks of CCaaS providers that offer verticalized solutions for those markets. However, it's neither necessary nor always the case. Because private clouds offer some cost savings and enjoy nearly the same scalability as public cloud, they appear as components of many CCaaS stacks.

The downside to choosing a vendor with a private cloud component is you're reliant on that vendor to implement security, change, and compliance practices. Large or mature CCaaS providers have the experience you need and have earned the trust of their customers in this regard. Be cautious of a new-to-the-market vendor that claims they can do it all themselves.

Do you want a vendor that's good at CCaaS or platform as a service (PaaS)? Mature companies have learned to do both. Smaller orgs are typically making a trade-off by the nature of their scale.

Hybrid Public and Private Clouds

Hybrid cloud is the latest of the three main architectures, emerging from two business necessities:

- Increased need for capacity flexibility, such as to support bursting during seasonal spikes
- Mitigation of the rising cost of public cloud

In a hybrid model, you can get the best of both worlds: rapid, dynamic scaling, and predictable cost control. This model allows CCaaS vendors to control their private cloud and recognize the inherent security advantages, while simultaneously being able to instantly scale via public cloud to handle spikes in traffic or interactions.

Come in for a Landing

All three cloud models provide vendors with a higher degree of flexibility, scalability, and cost savings over on-premises technology software, platforms, and infrastructure — which is how CCaaS providers can pass savings along to their clients. Hello economies of scale! However, since hybrid cloud bears the most benefits — the highest potential cost savings balanced against a high degree of control and risk mitigation — a vendor that includes both public and private components in its stack demonstrates thoughtful execution of its own cloud strategy. Look for this in a CCaaS provider.

Regardless of where the platform resides, ask the vendor these important questions:

- What's your disaster recovery plan?
- How will failovers work?
- Do you have in-region redundancy?
- Are you working with multiple public cloud and/or data center providers?

To be honest, the specifics of the responses are not as important as gauging whether the vendor has addressed all the contingencies. A vendor with hybrid infrastructure or capability of using multiple public clouds can offer maximum redundancy and will be your best bet in a partner vendor.

All that said, make sure the vendor you choose is truly committed to cloud. Some providers out there have a history of dabbling in the cloud: They'll launch a cloud offering, let it float for around a couple of years, launch another, and then discontinue the first one — forcing customers to migrate, again.

I recommend choosing a partner with a clear, committed cloud strategy — one who was either born in the cloud or who has a decades-long, unwavering, dedicated commitment to delivering all its services in the cloud. That way, you can trust that you'll know where your contact center will live. You don't want to try to build a house on a shifting foundation.

Crafting the Business Case

Let's pretend that you are ready and fully on team cloud. (Even if you aren't yet, I'm confident you'll get there by the end of the book.) Now let's pretend your C-level leadership team hasn't fully embraced the vision. You have a couple options: Subtly leave a copy of this book on their doorstep[5] or write up a killer business case to present to them.

Facts and numbers, baby. If we're going to sway an executive, we'll need good facts and numbers. I recommend making a spreadsheet that calculates conservative, likely, and best cases for the return. Break out costs over time (quarterly[6]), to clearly indicate when payment is due and when you'll realize value.

While the vendor might require up-front payment for the year, you might amortize the accounting by the month the services are delivered. A quick call to someone in finance can help identify the best way to account for these things and will help you impress the execs with astute financial forecasting.

Next, include details about how your model measures the return. Obviously, this will include the metrics, but more important are the assumptions you make while calculating the future metrics' value. For example, pretend one of your parameters involves the elimination of downtime with your new provider. Include all the facts and how downtime plays into your ROI model, such as the financial impact you experienced during your last outage and the new provider's historical/expected uptime.

---

[5] I find Amazon is an excellent passive-aggressive facilitator of anonymous gifts. :)

[6] Or whatever time period is appropriate for your business.

Another delta to call out explicitly is between theory and practice. For example, let's say the new application can automatically transcribe the call, summarize it, and log the summary into the CRM. After meeting with leaders inside the contact center, you've calculated that these tasks add up to 1,000 hours of manual work each month. And for the size of your center, that level of automation is a hefty return of time. But how much actual time do agents spend doing that today? Like in real life. It'd be nice if all calls received thorough documentation, and it would take 1,000 hours to do it, but today agents might spend only 40 hours taking mediocre notes. Do you calculate savings based on 40 hours or 1,000? I'd say you use 40 for true savings. But then extrapolate the value of that automation and the additional data it provides. That's where it's good to mention the 960 hours of free labor the system provides. Just put it in the "best case" column.

Many of the leaders I know like to dig into the numbers. So, consider providing the underlying mathematical model in a format or file they can manipulate. It's very possible they are privy to information that you don't have, which might influence some of your assumptions — like salaries, customer acquisition costs, etc.

Finally, summarize all your ideas in an executive summary. I'm a fan of written documents if they're under a half page. But consider using a presentation instead. You're in great shape if you can frame your ideas and make your numbers case using three or fewer slides. Just be prepared to provide all the details on demand. Facts and numbers, that's all it takes[7].

---

[7] If you want more help or don't feel up to the spreadsheet specifics, Blue Mesa Consulting and Forrester Research both offer reports that help quantify ROI. Search for "Total Economic Impact (TEI™) report" to explore Forrester's findings for your vendors of choice.

Why Now?

Cloud-based solutions have become the standard for delivering customer experience (CX) services. And 57.9% of consumers strongly agree that CX is a way for organizations to differentiate themselves from the competition[8]. The cloud offers the only sustainable path to deliver immediately relevant and truly dynamic customer experiences.

Regardless of size or industry, organizations are moving business processes to the cloud for the security, scalability, speed, and seamless omnichannel experiences it enables. If you're working to secure your position in this CX-driven world, moving the contact center to the cloud is not a question of if, but when.

PROCESS PIONEERS

Why Mark Chose the Cloud

Mark is an IT manager at a national food service equipment retailer. A single parent, he has worked in IT for over a decade but was new to the food service industry. He quickly found that his prior military experience helped him take on department logistics with a fresh angle that elevated client-customer relations. His overall goals when implementing CCaaS were to lower call-abandonment rates, reduce wait times, and increase customer satisfaction.

Mark: When I took on my role, I knew I would need to make systemic changes to allow our company to run more efficiently. As an IT manager, I inherited a contact center of about 200 agents that handled 26,000 calls each week on average. Our call-abandon rate was too high, and we had no way to measure client satisfaction with agent interaction.

---

[8] "2021 Global Customer Experience Benchmarking Report," Dimension Data, 2021.

Convincing the higher-ups to take on a company wide tech migration was initially a struggle. Everyone wants a solution, but no one wants the associated expense of time, money, or effort. I get it: Our company provides parts and services for multiple equipment brands and has more than 40,000 SKUs in stock for next-day delivery. With so many moving parts, it can seem that the only solution is to keep plugging away with whatever system you have in place, even if it is slowly destroying your business. There is simply no time to fix it.

I spent years in the military, where half the job was navigating procedural red tape, so I knew I would have to get creative.

We tried everything to improve our numbers: offering callbacks, redefining abandoned calls, adjusting schedules. Nothing seemed to work. And we had no way to measure our true problem. One day, it hit me during a routine visit to one of our branches: Because we didn't have contact options at the branches, everyone was rerouted to our national call center, which overwhelmed the agents. If we could open lines of communication without interrupting day-to-day operations, we could open the doors to new possibilities!

But our current setup didn't allow a way to integrate our branch and national call centers. As our company grew and opened new branches, our on-premises contact center held us back from providing the level of service our customers needed. After months of research and not-so-subtle hints to my supervisor that we could find a better solution, we got the go-ahead.

I knew CCaaS would be perfect. I stayed up all night preparing my pitch to my boss because I was so passionate about it. I'm always on the hunt for the most efficient way to handle any given problem, whether for my kids, my household, or my job. Efficiency means that our customers can spend less time on hold and our employees can solve issues more quickly, giving them more time off the phone.

About a week into our rollout, the pandemic hit. Our entire operation went remote, including our local branches, and we had only one or two personnel on-site at any given time. I felt like all the progress we had just made was about to fly out the window. How could we oversee a massive rollout with everyone in a different location across all sorts of time zones? Our vendor worked with us to retool everything to support a remote workforce. We experienced some growing pains with unreliable internet speeds and connectivity, but nothing some panicked calls and soothing reps couldn't solve.

Despite everything, we maaged to reduce our call-abandonment rate by more than 19% and achieved annual IT contact center savings of $100K. (Can you say bonus?!) Call volume has grown, and the number of agents has quadrupled even in a shifting economy. What's more, once our teams started returning to in-person work, our vendor helped us retool our systems to work for a hybrid scenario. Now, agents at the branches can take calls and provide the local experience our customers need in addition to the agents at our national call center.

Everyone — but most importantly my bosses — is happy! This project has been so successful, we've started thinking about what else we can put up into the cloud. Cloud for life, baby. Cloud for life!

CHAPTER THREE

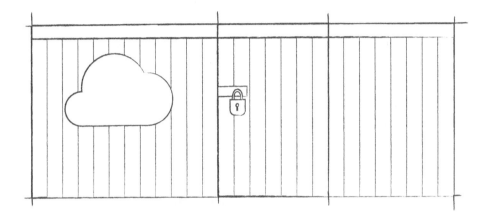

SECURING YOUR LAND

They say good fences make good neighbors. In business, strong security keeps the lights on and compliance keeps you out of jail. This chapter discusses trends in security, the costs of legal noncompliance, and the risks inherent with naïve choices in either topic. At the risk of stealing my own thunder, please pay special attention to the PCI, PII, and GDPR sections that follow: Non-compliance in those areas will cost your business the most.

Personal and Brand Reputational Risks

IT provides oversight for technology purchases, so you can't help but lend some of your personal reputation to the decisions. If you choose to remain on-premises, any challenges circle back to that decision and the team that manages the systems.

Likewise with cloud. When you move your contact center operations to the cloud, you effectively put your brand reputation in the hands of the vendor you select. If they get hacked, you get hacked. If they have an outage, you have an outage. If they do something stupid, you look foolish.

Luckily, subscription services depend on ongoing customer satisfaction. Preventing such episodes remains at the top of your vendor's priority list. Their survival depends on it. And specifically with respect to security, cloud solutions offer an economy of scale that you might not be able to achieve on your own on-prem. So, what you trade in control, you gain in horsepower.

Consider the story of Melissa, whose on-premises solution fell victim to hackers and how that affected her decision about moving to the cloud.

PROCESS PIONEERS

Melissa's Encounter with Hacker Hijinks

Melissa is a call center director for her county's public health department. She built her life in this town, feels passionate about serving her community, and takes her responsibility to heart. The experience delivered by some hacker hooligans gave her the opportunity to discover that same sense of community in an unexpected place: cloud contact center solutions.

Melissa: *Five minutes.* It took a hacker just five minutes to find their way into one of our servers and leave our organization — and all our patients — vulnerable.

I am a mother of four and have lived in my town for more than 30 years. The population is a beautiful mix of all walks of life while still having that small-town feel where you understand that you have the support of your neighbors.

Having devoted my life to public service, I work for a county public health department that employs more than 1,000 health professionals.

Our department used an on-premises contact center system and was in the initial stages of a five-year digital transformation strategy. We initially chose a slow rollout because, well, it's government, and things always seem to move slowly when there are processes and red tape involved. But we also wanted to give our employees ample time to adapt to a new system. It never occurred to me that we were opening ourselves up to security risks with a longer schedule.

When a tornado swept through our county, our old system couldn't scale fast enough to handle the spike in call volume. We found ourselves setting up temporary satellite offices to help support the aid efforts. The people answering our county healthcare hotline aren't traditional contact service agents, they're healthcare workers: nurses, physicians, and other staff. They need a system that's easy and flexible.

One morning at about 4 am, I got a call from the Director of Health Informatics and Technology. At that hour, I wasn't sure I was hearing him correctly. A hacker had managed to access one of our satellite office servers in the middle of the night. They dug around for five full minutes before IT caught their presence. IT immediately firewalled them, but there was no telling what damage they'd done in that time.

We manage an estimated budget of $70 million for 52 separately funded programs. It's taxpayer money, and our community deserves to always have its money and information secure. I felt violated on behalf of everyone in our county. We could no longer sacrifice security and leave our county vulnerable to a cyberattack.

IT leadership told us we were going to implement a new contact center solution. And we had to move quickly. The county's cybersecurity oversight committee gave us 48 hours to completely overhaul our system and migrate. I was stunned: It seemed impossible that our team of 1,000 could seamlessly transfer to something that we had initially planned would take five years!

The process couldn't have been easier. And our patients were thrilled because the new platform is simple to use. Soon we had a central line for natural disasters that we could dispatch at a moment's notice.

I was amazed that something so easy increased our security. What's more, it ended up saving money.

The platform is so flexible that once we got into it, we could see many possibilities to improve our systems. With a cloud-based solution, we had more flexibility to look at our workflows without the constraints of an on-premises system.

As a government entity, we're always looking to stretch taxpayer dollars. Shortly after setting up the natural disaster hotline, we began using the new tech for our IT help desk and Patient Access Center, which fields around 6,000 calls per month. Imagine applying the same level of security we had on our hotlines to every patient portal and database on our servers.

Our county may not be huge, but we are no less important and the people here matter. My neighbors are the most important people in my life, and working in public service makes it impossible for me not to care about their daily safety.

Alphabet Soup: Initialisms to Know

The contact center has its own vocabulary riddled with acronyms, initialisms, shorthand, and jargon. This list should help you sound like an expert during security and compliance conversations related to the contact center.

GDPR	Enforced by the EU's European Data Protection Board, the General Data Protection Regulation (GDPR) is designed to protect the privacy of EU residents. The regulation applies to both data controllers and data processors — entities that handle or collect personal data — regardless of whether the information is used for profit[9]. Penalties for noncompliance can cost up to 20 million euros or 4% of revenue. Yikes! There is a lot of subtlety to GDPR, but the essence is that individuals have the right to decide how you collect and use their data. And they have the authority to demand that you "forget" them. You can thank GDPR for the emergence of all the "accept cookies" popups in recent years.

---

[9] "CPRA vs. CCPA vs. GDPR: How the Difference Impacts Your Data Privacy Operations," WireWheel, 2022.

When shopping for a contact center vendor, this means two things: It must be compliant in how it handles their customers' (that means you) data appropriately and they must empower you to do the same for your customers. Part of their responsibility as a telecom provider will require them to collect CPNI (discussed below) data, so make sure they provide you a mechanism to initiate the "forgetting" process, in the event your EU-resident customers — even those living abroad — request it.

CCPA and CPRA

The California Privacy Rights Act (CPRA) enhances the California Consumer Protection Act (CCPA) by enforcing stricter protection of consumer privacy. It resembles GDPR, while adding requirements for businesses and applying to residents of the State of California in the United States. CCPA is responsible for the "do not sell my personal information" toggles now frequenting websites and mobile apps.

The impact of CCPA on the contact center is like that of GDPR. In addition to choosing a company that complies for your personal sake, make sure the vendor provides your team a way to automate the "opting out" process.

CPNI

Typically used in billing, customer proprietary network information (CPNI) refers to data that telecommunications services — like local, long-distance, and wireless carriers — acquire about their subscribers. Examples include what services subscribers use, as well as the amount and type of usage. The FCC regulates how organizations can use CPNI data.

Choose a vendor that has designed and implemented security and privacy controls to protect CPNI from unauthorized access or improper use. And one that doesn't sell CPNI to third parties or disclose CPNI without customer consent, except as required by law.

Cloud Security Alliance

The Cloud Security Alliance (CSA) is a nonprofit organization dedicated to defining and raising awareness of best practices to help ensure a secure cloud computing environment[10]. The collaboration of member organizations helps keep everyone safe by surfacing challenges and developing solutions that impact the data integrity of everyone. Some well-known member brands include Google, TD Bank, and IBM. Many enterprise-grade contact center solution providers are CSA members as well, a signal of their continued interest in and dedication toward security.

FCC

The US Federal Communications Commission (FCC) is the governing body for telecommunications. The FCC enforces many of the laws, acts, and regulations that follow. Contact center platforms that are registered carriers with the FCC may prove more

---

[10] https://cloudsecurityalliance.org/

knowledgeable and reliable when it comes to compliance to FCC regulations than vendors that white-label or resell the services of other registered carriers.

Fed RAMP

The Federal Risk and Authorization Management Program (FedRAMP) is a US federal government-wide program that provides a standardized approach to security assessment, authorization, and continuous monitoring for cloud products and services. While imperative for government clients, FedRAMP includes many specific requirements about data and employee residency that may not apply to your organization. Resist the urge to require every certification under the sun as you may inadvertently exclude vendors that specialize in servicing non-government clients.

HIPAA and HITECH

The Health Insurance Portability and Accountability Act (HIPAA) is a US federal law that protects sensitive patient health information from being disclosed without a person's consent or knowledge[11]. The Health Information Technology for Economic and Clinical Health (HITECH) Act, signed into law in 2009, promotes the adoption and meaningful use of health information technology[12]. The two

---

[11] Health Insurance Portability and Accountability Act of 1996, US Centers for Disease Control and Prevention. http://cdc.gov/phlp/publications/topic/hipaa.html

[12] HITECH Act Enforcement Interim Final Rule, US Department of Health & Human Services https://www.hhs.gov/hipaa/for-professionals/special-topics/hitech-act-enforcement-interim-final-rule/index.html

are closely related, but you will hear about HIPAA more often.

HIPAA becomes relevant to contact center applications that house health-related information. As a result, you'll often see contact center solutions prefer to remain a system processor for — not the home of — patient data. That is, they would rather handle the data in transit than replace your patient record-keeping application. Think of how you collect personal data during an IVA interaction or process it for real-time assistants. Integrate, don't absorb.

Still, you should evaluate how vendors handle the data whilst in transit. Is it written to a database? A log? How are those protected or purged? If you're a healthcare business or plan to serve healthcare customers inside your contact center, you may be subject to HIPAA regulations. Take the time to select a vendor that:

- Understands HIPAA and their responsibilities as the solution provider
- Is willing to sign a business associates' agreement (BAA) with your company

Together, that's a good indication that you're on the right path.

ISO/IEC 27001

ISO/IEC 27001 (ISO 27001, for short) is an international standard regarding the management of information security (infosec). Vendors that adopt international standards such as ISO 27001 demonstrate their commitment to security. ISO 27001 requires that management[13]:

- Systematically examine the organization's infosec risks, accounting for threats, vulnerabilities, and impacts
- Design and implement a coherent and comprehensive suite of infosec controls and/or other forms of risk treatment — such as risk avoidance or risk transfer — to address risks deemed unacceptable
- Adopt an overarching management process to ensure that infosec controls continue to meet the organization's information security needs on an ongoing basis

PCI a.k.a. PCI DSS

In 2006, American Express, Discover Financial Services, JCB International, MasterCard, and Visa Inc. formed the Payment Card Industry Security Standards Council — a global forum — to manage and guide the ongoing evolution of the Payment Card Industry Data Security Standard (PCI DSS)[14]. The guidelines govern the flow and security of credit card information. Any contact centers that collect payments from customers — whether by phone, via an automated system, or in a digital channel — are subject to these standards.

There are four levels of PCI compliance that correspond to a merchant's experience level and annual transaction volume. Level 1 merchants

---

[13] ISO/IEC 27001, Wikipedia

[14] https://www.pcisecuritystandards.org/

process more than 6 million transactions annually, while Level 4 handle fewer than 20,000. In addition, to become a Level 1 PCI DSS provider you need to obtain an attestation of compliance (AOC).

You're responsible for your own PCI level. Third-party validation that the vendor's practices, policies, and procedures meet or exceed the mark can save you the time of performing the checks yourself, but it doesn't mean your practices, policies, and procedures magically become compliant.

A contact center vendor might transact enough credit card payments for its own services to elevate it into a Level 1 status. But that doesn't guarantee it can support compliance for your organization's transactions on its platform. Keep in mind that compliance extends beyond the contact center application. For example, if your service team routinely records credit card information on sticky notes before entering it into a payment portal, you're not PCI-compliant. And no piece of contact center software will help.

So, choose a vendor with experience. One that knows how to handle its own transactions[15] and the transactions of its customers. Find a vendor with the AOC to prove its compliance and one that isn't afraid to (unofficially) point out any noticeable compliance flaws in your center. Expect the vendor's sales team to speak from a place of experience and help you design a solution that fits both your business and the law.

---

[15] The vendor's own transactions could include them taking credit card payment for their products and services.

SOC 2 Type 2

Service Organization Control 2 relates to certain organizational controls related to elements such as security, availability, processing, and privacy. SOC 2 Type 2 reports on the internal controls of a company. It captures how a company safeguards customer data and how well those controls operate. If you've chosen to use a cloud service provider for your contact center, find one that uses SOC 2 reports to assess and address the risks associated with their technology services. These reports, issued by independent third-party auditors, cover the principles of security, availability, confidentiality, and privacy. Since they're issued after a year of evaluation, pursuing such a certification demonstrates the vendor's commitment to security in the following areas:

- Infrastructure: The physical and hardware components — networks, facilities, equipment — that support their platform or solution
- Software: The operating software and programs — utilities, applications, systems — that comprise the solution itself
- People: The personnel — managers, users, developers, etc. — involved in the security, management, governance, and operations of delivering services to customers
- Data: The information — interaction data, files, databases, transaction streams, etc. — used by the service
- Procedures: The manual or automated procedures that pull it all together

TCPA

The US Congress passed the federal Telephone Consumer Protection Act (TCPA) in response to increasing consumer complaints about telemarketer and debt-collector phone calls. TCPA restricts the making of telemarketing calls, the use of automatic dialing systems, and use of artificial or prerecorded voice messages. Assessed on a per-call basis, the fines for noncompliance add up quickly.

Unfortunately, several companies have made a business of trying to catch organizations that are out of compliance with TCPA. One tactic they use is to complete online "contact me" forms and wait for a call from an auto-dialer system. If the form's language doesn't include opt-in verbiage, the call can be illegal, even if the recipient signed up for contact.

If an arm of your organization already makes automated outbound dials, they're aware of the nuance of TCPA. However, if you suspect a team is considering adding a new sales team in the contact center or wants to explore blending inbound interactions with proactive outbound communication, it's worth a conversation with your compliance officer.

To simplify the process — and preserve your future options — look for a solution with a variety of dialing strategies, including at least one that's specifically TCPA compliant. And use caution when taking direction from your outbound sales team leadership as they may have a more creative, less-restrictive interpretation of the law that they may use to disqualify truly compliant solutions. Finally, look for a vendor that offers third-party opinions on the compliance status of their dialers. Lawyers with telecom compliance expertise or firms like CompliancePoint are great places to start.

PROCESS PIONEERS

The Time Matt Almost Went to Jail

Matt is the contact center vice president for a US private cable and home automation service provider. He is also a husband and a father of two who lives for his family. One of his toughest moments in life was when his company failed an external compliance audit and he had 72 hours to fix it or risk jail time.

Matt: When I first learned that our company was undergoing an external audit, I was a bit concerned but not worried. I knew there might be some issues because we hadn't updated our contact center platform recently, but it wasn't anything that we couldn't fix easily.

I was in for a shock.

I suspected something was wrong when the auditor first requested to talk with our CEO. They were in his office for an hour. When they finally emerged, our CEO's face was sullen. I remember thinking, "This is it. I'm getting fired!"

The CEO called me to his office and showed me the audit report. Bad would be an understatement: It was a disaster.

"We're in violation of about every regulation," my CEO said. "We are not looking at just potential penalties. You could go to jail. Do you have any idea how damaging this could be to our business reputation?"

I knew too well what had happened: I was too trusting. I'm the first to admit that I'm no compliance expert. It's hard enough just to keep up with the names of all the regulations; you also must know the provisions within each one.

And the regulations continuously add new provisions and change existing ones.

I'd rather delegate the compliance tasks to the experts so that I can focus on making sure the contact center provides the best customer service. So, when tasked to ensure our contact center was compliant, I brought in a team of "experts." Unfortunately, they missed a few critical things.

For one, our current system failed to properly implement the "pause recording" functionality when customers made purchases by phone, which exposed their financial details. We were also secretly listening to and recording calls as part of agent performance evaluations, which is technically illegal eavesdropping. I wish the team that had configured the application had mentioned the need to notify callers with an audio disclaimer.

Moreover, in an attempt to increase efficiency, I created automated calls that turned out to be a TCPA violation prohibiting pre-recorded telemarketing calls. It's beyond me why our account manager let us deploy that solution after I described my intent.

Things were not looking good.

"Did you say I could go to jail?" I asked the CEO coming out of my initial shock. My mind was now on my family. How would they cope with me in jail? My firstborn looked up to me as an idol, but he has the grit of a tiger: He'd probably be inspired to become a lawyer so that he could defend people like me. I was most worried about Meg, my youngest.

After collecting myself, I sat down with the CEO and the auditor to explore our options. The auditor agreed that we hadn't blatantly tried to undermine the regulations. And while ignorance is not an excuse, our CEO agreed that the company would stand behind me. The auditor gave us a chance to set things right: We had 72 hours to get into compliance before the auditor had to report the findings.

It was the longest three days of my life.

I knew what we had to do. It started with replacing our current contact center. The challenge was finding the right solution backed by experts who deeply understood the compliance landscape. And we were clearly operating on a deadline.

After hours of research and consultation with people in my network, one solution looked like a winner. I read a case study about how the vendor helped another firm set up its contact center in just 48 hours. I immediately scheduled a call.

After explaining my predicament and sharing the audit report, the rep took me through a step-by-step process of how they would solve my problem. Even with my limited compliance knowledge, I knew this vendor could save us (particularly, me).

The system was up and running two days later. And my job was no longer in peril. The benefits of the new contact center extended beyond our compliance issue. It significantly increased efficiency by handling more calls, reducing abandoned calls, and lowering operational costs. The platform integrated with Microsoft Dynamics and had multiple communication channels, allowing us to leverage email and chat as well as voice.

It's easy to look back and laugh now. But those three days were incredibly stressful. The hardest part was keeping everything secret from my family. A month later I finally told them the full story.

Guess what my son told me? "Dad, when I grow up, I want to be a lawyer so that innocent people like you don't have to worry about jail." My wife's response wasn't as friendly, lol. Now I appreciate the criticality of partnering with a vendor that has my best interests in mind. It's a lesson I will never forget.

CHAPTER FOUR

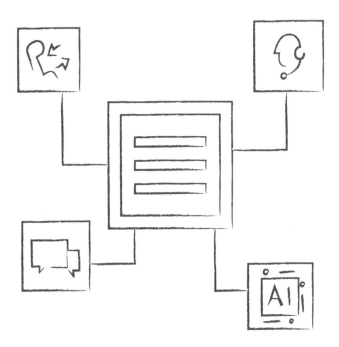

BRINGING IN THE UTILITIES

Before breaking ground on any dream home, you must first address the infrastructure for your utilities. Verifying that you'll have the electricity, water, and gas lines to keep your home warm, well lit, and perfectly watered is paramount. If they're unavailable in the area, your project will slow (at the very least), and your result will fail to meet expectations.

When it comes to your contact center, utilities represent all the other business applications and telephony upon which your contact center directly or indirectly depends.

Ask yourself questions like:

- Where does the customer data live?
- How should the contact center contribute to the corporate data lake?
- What is our AI strategy?
- Who will our telephony carrier be?
- Should we bring our own telephony?

Don't sweat an incomplete requirements list. It's not a tragedy if you end up having to dig a well in the backyard because one day someone decides to add an unplanned hot tub. But you don't want little water holes scattered all over the property because you didn't choose a solution that supported the spirit of your agile business philosophy.

The Importance of Third-Party Applications

Some argue that a contact center is only as strong as the data behind it. I'd agree. Sure, many contact center–related business decisions will stem from contact center data. But the system itself can't run on self-generated information alone; it also needs a steady supply of customer information.

Customer data is typically scattered among several applications including CRM, enterprise resource planning (ERP), e-commerce, web, and other — sometimes bespoke — data sources. During contact center interactions, all this data needs a place to come together to provide a holistic view of the customer.

At this phase of the purchasing decision, you don't have to worry about the specific locations of every bit of data the contact center needs to service customers. (We'll discuss specifics later.) But you do need to ensure the solution you choose can accommodate important, broad-stroke requirements including:

- Can the application connect to web services easily?
- Do your customer information systems have web services?

- Are there documented APIs and pre-built integrations for your applications?
- Does the vendor have a strong track record of successful integration projects?
- Does the vendor offer different user experiences for organizations with and without a separate CRM system?

The last question might seem a little out of place, but screen real estate comes at a premium. Some business units might want to go full tilt on a new single-pane-of-glass experience, while others will prefer to have their teams work from the comfort of a familiar CRM application. And you will want to provide them with options.

If you have multiple business units, also confirm that the vendors can support different integrations, adapters, and user experience choices by business unit. One size does not fit all, and one contact center can serve many departments.

Corporate Storage and Data Lakes

The sources that feed data into your contact center are just as important as where contact center data goes at the end of the process. Any solution worth purchasing should come with advanced reporting features that support your desire to dig in and explore your data.

And they should be intuitive enough that line-of-business teams can do their own reporting. As an IT professional, you have better things to do. Better things like making sure all the data ends up in your corporate storage and related data lakes.

IT is the glue in the contact center of the future. You take the insights gleaned from one area of the business and apply them to other areas. And you can't do it without looking at the big picture, which means correlating contact center data with the other data available in your enterprise.

At this phase of your selection, ensure that simple, automated data dumps are feasible. Make sure you can both receive the information via a push or use available APIs to pull it — just in case.

AI Readiness

Even following a 270%[16] growth spurt for AI adoption inside the contact center between 2016 and 2019 and continued year-over-year growth of 25%[17] since then, almost four in five (79%) of contact centers surveyed in 2022 plan to increase spending in AI this year[18]. As more organizations get on the "AI train," not having an AI and automation strategy becomes a risk to your core business.

We will discuss different types of AI technology and their roles in the contact center in the Smart Home section of the Selecting a Furniture Package chapter. At this stage in the buying process, you simply want to make sure the AI utilities are available for service. Ask:

- Does the vendor have a clear AI strategy?
- Is the AI technology proprietary or best of breed? Or both?
- Has the vendor taken steps to simplify administration and training of the AI?
- Can you plug in third-party AI engines?
- What is the vendor's AI partner strategy?

---

[16] "Gartner Survey Shows 37 Percent of Organizations Have Implemented AI in Some Form," Gartner, January 2019.

[17] "The Call Center AI Market To Expand At A 25% Growth Rate With The Rising Demand For AI-Based Intelligent Virtual Assistants As Per The Business Research Company's Call Center AI Global Market Report 2022," The Business Research Company, July 2022.

[18] "The future of AI 2022: Progressing AI maturity in the contact center," Talk desk Research™ Report, 2022.

Why Serena Had to Start Over, Again

Serena has worked as an IT director for a successful non-profit for many years. Recently, her organization merged with an acquired nonprofit that, while successful, was struggling to bring its digital infrastructure into the 21st century. Attempting to merge both systems proved to be a disastrous experience and taught her many important lessons about digital integration.

Serena: The past few years at my job were quite a rollercoaster ride. About 10 years ago, I started at this wonderful nonprofit that builds and manages low-cost housing for people across the state of Georgia. We were a ragtag group of people who were all motivated by the desire to do good and see our communities thrive regardless of economic situation. When I started, we provided services to a little over 2,000 individuals. I watched that number grow right up until a few years ago when we merged with another company, and that number doubled overnight. Now, we manage more than 20,000 homes and service over 50,000 people.

The merge was extremely rocky from both the personnel and IT perspectives. I wish I could say that I was a fearless leader throughout the process, but I was terrified. As with most mergers, we found ourselves with several redundancies, and many of us were stressed about keeping our jobs. Fortunately, I was promoted to be the IT director for the entire operation. While I wanted to celebrate, I knew I needed to get to work immediately to prove I was the right choice. My IT manager and I spent a couple of weeks getting to know both operations and identifying possible ways to integrate the systems. Hoping to avoid the stressors of a company-wide migration to a completely new system, we decided our best path forward was to have both teams remain on their respective platforms and integrate them so that each "side" could teach the other one. Sounds perfect, right?

Three months in, we were floundering. Our initial strategy was experiencing a glorious crash and burn. Our IT team was unable to keep up with all the bugs and glitches that appear when you try to merge two systems that were never meant to work together. What's worse, we realized that the other organization was using multiple systems to manage client contact information and never had a central solution. It was utter chaos. I felt like I had failed and made the mess we had inherited even worse.

My team and I realized we needed better integration capabilities. We researched many vendors but were impressed by the integration capabilities of the one we chose, plus all the other solutions it had to streamline our work.

Our first step was to implement the contact center for customer interactions. We saw an immediate boost to the morale of the agents and managers, who quickly acknowledged the benefits of the system's functionality in their daily tasks. It integrated seamlessly with both CRMs, giving our teams detailed information about customers, their call history, and their individual needs.

For me, the big selling point was the ability to replace several regional telephone numbers with one central point of contact. And we could keep things simple for our existing customers. We published our new numbers externally but automatically routed calls to the previous numbers to our centralized queue. It's so much simpler to have all the calls go to the same place.

We can also integrate voice, chat, and email communications for a seamless customer experience. And when we're ready for AI, we can go there too. Going in, I was worried that we'd face resistance from employees about having to learn an entirely new system, but everyone was thrilled to have all the customer data they need at their fingertips. None of our data is getting lost and it's clearly laid out for every agent to find with a click of their mouse.

Porting vs. BYOT

It can be tempting to want to bring your own telephony carrier (BYOT) to the cloud with you. Maybe you have an existing relationship that represents many years. You might have a mind-blowingly low per-minute rate. Or you're just stuck with a multiyear agreement that your predecessor signed. Whatever your motivation to consider that path, let's look at the options so you can make the best decision for the business.

You Get What You Pay For

A low per-minute rate represents only one part of the total cost of telephony. Sure, you want a competitive price, but you also want your customers to be able to reach you. And if you're making outbound calls, you want those numbers to have a good reputation and a quality connection. Ask your carriers what they're doing to preserve your number reputation, prevent numbers from being marked as spam, and what kind of backup and redundancy they offer with that great per-minute pricing.

Resilience

If I had a nickel for every time a customer said a stiff wind and a weak tree branch took out their telephony, I wouldn't need to write this book. (Wait, yes, I would... nickels don't buy you much anymore. But you get the idea.) Relying on a single carrier represents a single point of failure. If that carrier experiences issues in a particular region, you might not have the luxury of moving your traffic to another carrier. At least not with the ease that a quality cloud contact provider can deliver.

When looking for a provider, choose one that:

- Works with multiple carriers, both large and small
- Has a clear, documented practice of monitoring traffic and routing calls away from problem networks and onto performant ones
- Can provide carrier redundancy and the peace of mind that comes with 24x7 network operations support
- Has a proven track record and customer testimonials to back up its claims

Why leave all your eggs in a single basket like a high school student trying to learn to appreciate the responsibility of parenthood[19]? When instead you can outsource that headache and know that if something goes wrong, your vendor will resolve it without you having to worry about it.

---

[19] "Egg Baby Project Ideas," Study.com, accessed October 2022.

CHAPTER FIVE

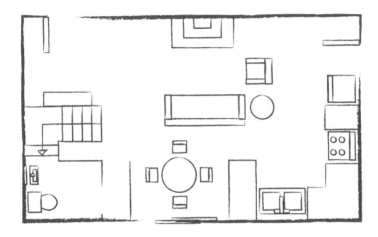

DESIGNING THE BUILDING(S)

By now you should, philosophically, know where you want to build your dream home. You've selected the plot of land, decided on the view, and made sure that you can hook up to the utilities.

Now it's time to design. What's the primary function of your home? Are you building to house a family, entertain your friends, or simply to create a tranquil oasis for yourself? It's the same for the contact center. Consider who your contact center will serve. Identify your primary goals or use cases: Are you emphasizing sales, marketing, support, inbound, outbound — or building to support all of the above?

As an IT professional, you're used to juggling the demands of multiple business leaders. With priorities and budgets differing from team to team, you have an opportunity to add real value to the organization at this phase of the evaluation process. You have insights into the needs of the whole business, giving you an invaluable perspective you can put to work.

Contact center projects typically manifest in one of three ways:

- A business unit's needs are not being fulfilled by the current solution
- New needs arise, and a team emerges requiring a contact center solution
- The organization decides to make the strategic decision to improve its technology stack

In the first two buying scenarios, IT isn't always involved. Or when you are, you're not brought in until late in the buying cycle. Some organizations prefer it this way. If your business has clearly established buying guides that support business units shopping independently, cool. We suggest you consider using the lessons contained in this book to create a "go-by" document that can help shoppers consider the more nuanced aspects of the purchase. By doing so, you'll create rapport and increase the likelihood of inclusion in future purchase considerations.

If, on the other hand, your business (rightfully, in my opinion) considers the contact center as a strategic component of the overall business, there's a good chance that your team is driving the project. If not, take the steps necessary to involve yourself as early as possible.

Who Counts as an Agent?

Think of the contact center as the digital "front door" of your business. People may enter that door via a variety of channels; most often by phone — although that's changing[20]. So, when trying to

---

[20] From 2007 to 2022, inbound voice interactions as a percentage of the total inside the contact center fell from ~83% to ~75%, having been replaced by email, chat, and social media. Source: ContactBabel US Contact Centers 2022-2026 The State of the Industry & Technology Penetration 9th edition

figure out who in your organization "counts" as a contact center agent, a good place to start is by asking yourself: Who in the business has a phone?

Naturally, not everyone with a phone or headset on their desk is a contact center agent. So next consider: When someone calls and Jim's phone rings, are they expecting to speak to Jim specifically? Or just someone like Jim? If the answer is "someone like Jim," then that person is a good candidate for the contact center solution — even if they don't consider themselves an agent.

Next, we'll want to consider the people who speak to customers on non-voice channels.

- Does your company use web chat? What about social media or business messaging tools like Facebook or WhatsApp?
- Who responds to text messages (SMS) sent to the company's phone numbers?
- Who handles email?

Robots count in this evaluation. If you send automatic reminder texts, for example, that's an interaction, even if replies receive a default "no one monitors this mailbox" message. Count it because it represents an opportunity to improve the customer experience.

Extend Beyond the Contact Center

Now that you have a good list of who and how people connect with customers, think about who your employees need to speak to. Draw a circle around all the direct-touch, customer-facing employees that you identified. Now draw a second circle outside the first one. We'll fill this circle with people who help the contact center folks succeed.

For the employees who interact with the outside world, who are the internal teams they need to speak with to accomplish their day-to-day activities? For example, if a customer calls support about a billing problem, does the agent need to conference in a billing department employee to resolve the issue? If so, include billing as a department of interest in that second circle. We'll refer to members of this second circle as "back office" workers.

Look at Internal Services

Finally, in a third circle, think about your internal support teams and the activities they perform to keep the business running.

- Does your IT department have a help line? Does IT return calls to employees who enter tickets?
- Does HR have a contact process for benefits or grievances?
- Does sales operations support contracts or otherwise help a large field sales organization?
- Does facilities have a ticketing system for requests for over-zealous air conditioning systems or printer malfunctions?

All these departments can benefit from the AI, automation, intelligent routing, accountability, and enablement solutions available from modern contact center solutions.

Supporting Several Lines of Business

Now that we know who we can help, let's talk about what we need from a vendor solution to accommodate the diversity of processes it will support.

Billing and Budget

How does your business handle billing? Does IT own the budget? Do you charge back to the individual lines of business? If one business unit owns the contract, does it need funds transferred from peer departments? Whichever the case, the ability to provide billing at the business-unit level — both for licensing and long-distance costs — will save you time and headache in the long term.

Administration and Reporting

If multiple business units share a solution, you'll want to carefully consider the permission structure. Does the solution use a zero-trust permission policy where people can perform only a specific set of explicitly assigned functions? Can you segment roles into tiers to manage feature access? Does the solution provide a mechanism to segment the data for reporting? Can you design different customer experiences separately? How do auditing and change logging work?

Not every answer will be 100% to your liking; no vendor is perfect. But balance the related tradeoffs with the time and effort you'll save by choosing a solution that fits your business model.

The Appeal of the "Lift and Shift"

Speaking of business models, beware of the "lift and shift." When seeking requirements from your business partners, many will get caught in a mental loop of "we do it this way, therefore this is how it must be done." Other thought-trapping logic will refer to "year-over-year numbers" and — please! — revisit anything that currently takes more than four clicks to accomplish.

People don't like change. But in my experience, that's not the primary source of the "lift and shift" attitude. Deep down they want change; they know something new will bring better features and novel possibilities. Yet after selecting a tool with top-notch technology, they still ask for the same old implementation. Why? Because creativity is harder than change.

Have you ever sat in front of a bucket of LEGO® building blocks without an instruction booklet? Be honest. How interesting was that rectangle-of-a-house you built? People know what they know and stick to the familiar, especially if admitting they don't have an answer might mean people perceive them as less than an expert.

This is good news. You get to function as an unbiased observer. A solution architect. You can be the agent of change that the business units need to help them imagine their world from a fresh perspective. You get to add measurable business value. By putting your stamp on this project early, you can define your role as a strategic partner and not just another person who needs to sign off. Take this opportunity. It can change your career path.

But I Don't Like Change Either — And I'm No Good at Puzzles

Don't sweat if you don't immediately see how all the pieces fit together. You have help. I'm here to give you a good start, and vendors are often eager to assist. They know contact center solutions have robust feature sets, multiple ways to accomplish similar tasks, and experience assisting the work preferences of several users. Vendors should also provide sample use cases for your specific vertical. While seldom comprehensive, these examples will help illustrate the "art of the possible."

To be better, you must first be different.

Help your team explore the art of the possible by asking questions like the following:

- What are you trying to accomplish?
- What agent and/or customer behavior do you need to change? Or preserve and, even, encourage?
- How do you believe your current processes hinder your desired outcomes?

Climb Out of the Weeds

During this exercise you will undoubtably encounter someone who's so focused on the way things are that they won't make it hard to escape the fine details. You'll get very tactical responses to "what are you trying to accomplish?"

It's like a pinball player telling you that "the ball has to come off this paddle at precisely 35 degrees." They've been playing a particular machine for years and settled on 35 degrees as the optimal paddle-to-ball contact angle. They're so settled that they're convinced that it's the only acceptable angle. In their universe, this capability is of the utmost importance, and they won't accept a solution (new machine) without it.

If you ask someone what they're trying to accomplish and receive a response of: "to get the ball to bounce at a 35-degree angle," it might sound like a reasonable answer. It's not. A real answer focuses on the end goal. Our pinball player's answer should more like: "I'm trying score lots of points" or "to get more tickets."

Even those replies fail to tell the full story. Because the actual reason they want those points is something like: "I want the new high score" and "I want to impress my partner with a giant stuffed animal," respectively.

Similarly, inside the contact center, when it comes to reporting, some people love lists and others prefer colors and lines. Both are valid approaches, but the goal is to understand the business so they can adapt and improve, not have a specifically periwinkle icon on the graph. The more mired in the weeds your business partners are, the more value you can add. You just need to get comfortable with asking "why" an annoying number of times. Think gold. The more you dig, the more lucrative the ultimate outcomes. So, dig in!

It can help to mix up the ways you ask the question. Try some of these options:

- What happens if we do it differently?
- How do you intend to use the results? (Especially good for reporting mandates.)
- What could improve if we did it differently?
- Whose expectations do changes affect?
- What would break if we made a change?

And my personal favorite: "What happens if we don't change anything?"

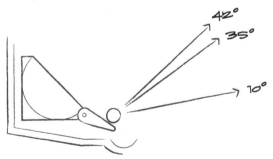

Going back to the pinball example earlier, the conversation might go something like this:

> **You:** Why do you need a 35-degree ball angle?
>
> **Pinball Wizard:** Because it's the best.
>
> **You:** What makes it the best?
>
> **Pinball Wizard:** The results — the ball goes exactly where I want it.
>
> **You:** Why do you want the ball to go there?
>
> **Pinball Wizard:** Because that spot scores points.
>
> **You:** How many points are you trying to score?
>
> **Pinball Wizard:** All of them.
>
> **You:** Sure, but do you have a goal in mind? What does success look like?
>
> **Pinball Wizard:** Top high score.
>
> **You:** Cool. What if I told you that other players, including the current leader, used 10-degree and 42-degree angled hits to reach their scores. And they did so in less time than you've been standing here. Would you consider a solution that had those options?

There's a good chance your sales rep already tries to do this. So, use them, or simply let them. That way they can be the initial "why bad guy," and you can observe the line of questioning and think about how the responses impact the business beyond the specific use case.

Your goal is to identify opportunities to suggest changes and improvements — and to stop business partners from recreating the same problematic "solution" they already have. Don't use new parts to replicate an old toy. It's time to upgrade, so upgrade.

Phased vs. All-at-Once Approaches

While it's important to understand the potential scope of a project before you select a vendor, you don't need to iron out every detail before you begin. An architect doesn't need you to select a sofa before they draw the plans, because — like we're doing here

— they take it one step at a time. For this reason, I recommend taking a phased approach.

Aside from simplifying project management, a phased approach gives your team learning opportunities as you go. You gain valuable experience as each new business unit, service, or customer experience goes live on the new platform. The perspective you gain as you familiarize yourself with the implementation process and the product itself helps shape subsequent implementations. Your team can adapt their requirements and vision for how the future contact center will look.

Think of it like designing your new house room by room. Like a group of naïve business leaders, your youngest child might beg for a hot pink room. Despite suspecting that they will quickly outgrow their affinity for the color, you relent and let the youngest (smallest team) move forward with the paint. In doing so, the older kids realize that — while they like it — it might not be the best long-term choice. Seeing things in action helps people make better design choices going forward.

And, if the pink walls totally work, you'll start realizing ROI very quickly and will know how to paint the other rooms even more efficiently. Either way, each subsequent team benefits from the experiences of those who came before them. So, map out phases. In a contact center transition, patience makes perfect — but if you don't get started, you'll be left behind.

IN A CONTACT CENTER TRANSITION, PATIENCE MAKES PERFECT — BUT IF YOU DON'T GET STARTED, YOU'LL BE LEFT BEHIND.

Why Grant Phased His Implementation

Grant was an IT "whiz kid" who was scouted by his company to implement drastic operational improvement solutions and bring the business into the modern era. His drive to modernize the workplace, however, will never get in the way of his slow and steady methodology that has allowed him to excel throughout his career.

Grant: I work for one of the UK's largest privately owned property services companies specializing in the social housing, education, and commercial sectors. We deliver innovative planned and responsive repairs nationally and work in more than 400,000 homes a year. We focus on property maintenance and improvement, both planned and reactive; painting and redecoration; passive fire protection; and compliance services.

I joined about two years ago to modernize our operations and bring them into the 21st century. My resume was full of similar IT overhauls at previous companies, and our company had struggled with outdated operational solutions for several years. I was excited to take on this new challenge. I'd never worked with a company whose legacy was this renowned.

I could tell from my first week that everyone wanted change yesterday and was ready to dive in, even though no one had a full grasp on the level of undertaking it would require. My company has been around since the 1940s. It has an extremely diverse portfolio of business offerings that had increased over the years, but never built into the company operations in a cohesive way. We had a wide range of needs we had to address. It felt a bit like entering a baby in a marathon: We weren't even crawling yet, but the business wanted to run.

I also worried about compliance. We have entire teams dedicated to meeting building regulations and ensuring our properties are up to code, but everyone seemed naive to the details of consumer compliance. If we opened the gates to all these new technologies for our employees, would we fall out of compliance and face hefty fines? It was the last thing we needed, especially after such a tumultuous year for our economy.

I decided to pull the reins in a bit and urge the executive board to phase our operations overhaul for the sake of my team's sanity, and that of the entire company. We figured it would be best to start with a clear picture of our end goal, then roll everything out in stages. We picked the area that needed the most help first: our contact centre.

We wanted to move to a cloud contact centre solution that could integrate with our job management system and help us better manage customer service. It was crucial that the solution met stringent privacy and security restrictions while still allowing for ease of use and flexibility. Our core market is social housing, and we work closely with the government, so there was no margin for error. Fortunately, our vendor ensured we never lost track of any policies we have to follow and has its own team monitoring changes to government consumer policies, which takes a huge burden off of us.

Within a month of implementing phase one, we noticed the benefits of the improved call routing straight away. We plan to migrate more of our legacy solutions, but the ability to integrate with a lot of our existing solutions simplified the first phase.

With better call routing, reporting capabilities, and real-time displays, our supervisors and service desk managers can manage their teams more effectively and streamline their processes. We've been able to win more contracts due to our contact centre improvements — and having this under our belt has emboldened us to make more drastic IT changes in the future.

We are continuing to look for ways to improve. We just completed phase two, which includes gamification. I'm excited to see how it makes work more engaging and empowering for agents. Phase three will take us to more geographies to support our expansion into Germany. Applying what we learned during our initial implementations will ensure that the project goes even smoother.

Identifying Impacted Geographies

To fully appreciate the scope of the geographic regions your contact center engages with, you'll need to evaluate the world from a few different perspectives. First, consider any region of the world where you have customers. Then ask where the customers move to — are they residents of Europe, but live in Canada, for example. Next flip the lens and see where you have agents or other contact center staff. Finally consider all the places, countries, and regions where the data or telecom pass through. Taken collectively, those become what I call your impacted geographies.

Where Are Your Customers?

The geographies impacted by contact center investment might reach beyond areas in which you market or sell. For example, a company that sells spelunking equipment might market only to people in Canada, but its customers use the equipment to explore caves all over the world. So, customers call for support from overseas. The question becomes: Does this company make it easy — or even possible — for customers to reach them from overseas?

To identify where you customers are, figure out both where they live and — depending on how people use your product or service — where they go.

Language-Related Legal Requirements

Is it legally required for you to provide customers with service in a local language? Going back to the Canadian spelunking company example, depending on its retail sales office locations and the regions in which its target customers reside, the company might have a legal obligation to provide service in French and English. Your business units know the requirements of regions where they currently do business, but as someone in the organization with visibility into corporate expansion plans, use your perspective to anticipate and research regional requirements. Then ensure your vendor can help you support those initiatives.

Country Residency Requirements

Some countries require registration of phone numbers to specific individuals or addresses. Italy, for example, requires registering phone numbers issued inside the country to a passport to align with VoIP regulations that ensure accountability for any nefarious number use. Now, I'm sure you would never use a phone number issued for business inappropriately. But do you think Andrew in accounting would happily use his passport number to become officially accountable for the contact center's usage of a number?

The point: Don't take number accessibility for granted. If you ask potential vendors if they can provide numbers in Italy, they will say yes. But does your team have the local resources to satisfy the regulatory requirements of the numbers being issued to them? Maybe not. Sometimes it's about having a local point of contact; other times you'll need a physical office presence. While cloud does make it easy to issue numbers anywhere, local regulations still add occasional complexity. No mountain is unsurmountable; you just need a plan.

No MOUNTAIN IS
UNSURMOUNTABLE;
YOU JUST NEED A PLAN.

Feature Availability

The cloud helps businesses and vendors alike innovate very quickly. Many cloud vendors release new features every week. But they don't necessarily release them everywhere, all at once. Regulatory reasons may mean they need to "slow-roll" certain features across their global network.

To avoid surprises down the road, specifically ask your vendor to confirm that all the services you think you're subscribing to are available in the regions you need them.

And don't fret if they're not. Many vendors are happy to work with you to bring their capabilities to market in new regions. They might not currently support a particular region simply because no one ever asked them to. Supply and demand. There's no sense in keeping a light on in a room no one uses, right?

Remember that as a part of your phased implementation, a cloud vendor can typically move at the speed of business and meet you there when you're ready. The important thing is to ask the questions and jointly craft a plan.

Where Is Your Staff?

In the office? At home? On a boat? Cloud may make it easy to have agents "anywhere," but you still need to figure out where people will work when designing your contact center dream home. This exercise will help you understand where and what kind of dedicated virtual private network (VPN) or MPLS circuits make sense, or if they make sense at all. It will also help you begin to design — or at least plan for — call routing plans. Will you follow the sun or follow the language[21]? Do you have customers in places or regions not well-covered by your existing staffing model? If so, it might make sense to hire some remote employees to fill the gaps.

Considerations for Remote Workers

The pandemic accelerated the remote work trend, and it appears to be here to stay. While having remote workers comes with many business benefits (cost savings, employee satisfaction, etc.), supporting a remote contact center workforce can put strain on IT. The following considerations will help alleviate these potential pains.

Consideration #1: Candidate Selection

"Open a Chrome browser." That's a phrase anyone reading this book probably takes for granted. But in the process of going remote, one of the companies I worked with quickly realized not everyone on its staff was so hip to the lingo. So, consideration #1 for hiring a remote workforce: Select candidates who are easy for your teams to support. Work with your business units to ensure their employees possess the requisite knowledge to access your systems and training with ease.

Consideration #2: Endpoint Testing

Your business unit brethren will worry about all the on-the-job training it takes to help them service clients. And they'll come to your team to troubleshoot call quality. But if you choose a cloud provider, you may not have access to your favorite testing tools. That's okay. As we've covered, it's best to focus on outcomes over tactics when making a big change. Evaluate potential vendors on their ability to provide you with endpoint monitoring at the agent level and how easy they make it to resolve quality.

---

[21] Some providers offer real-time translation solutions which can make following the language easier.

Consideration #3: Thin-Client Support

Does the platform vendor support your thin-client environment? Does it certify the solution on all the virtual desktop infrastructure (VDI) environments your business uses? And if your existing VDI environment is a bit dusty, does the vendor support the options you're considering for an upgrade?

Consideration #4: VPNs

You might encounter the term "tromboning" as you shop for contact center solutions. Used to describe unnecessarily long data paths, tromboning refers to how you can elongate the path of the sound waves inside a trombone by extending the instrument's slide.

To avoid unnecessary tromboning of your voice path — and suffering the associated poor voice quality — we recommend *split tunneling*[22] for remote uses. Clever use of split tunneling will allow your encrypted (by the provider) voice to remain in-region, where it will enjoy the shortest path and lower latency. At the same time, it allows your less time-sensitive business applications — like CRM screen pops — to "phone home" over the corporate VPN.

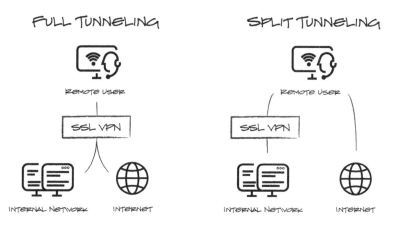

Figure 6-1: VPN Tunneling Options

---

[22] Split tunneling is a VPN feature that divides your internet traffic, sending some through an encrypted VPN tunnel while routing the rest through a separate tunnel on the open network.

Consideration #5: Support

Finally, make sure you understand who supports agent connectivity issues. With workers scattered all over the city, country, or globe, troubleshooting individual connectivity issues can become overwhelming for IT organizations that are unaccustomed to that level of remote support. It's unlikely that the vendors you evaluate will chomp at the bit to assume ownership themselves but should be willing to work with your team to isolate the issue.

We recommend you plan to have your internal IT team field calls for basic connectivity/sound quality issues. They can do simple troubleshooting to help identify if the issue is isolated to the remote worker or related to the worker's internet service provider (ISP). Once you've ruled out the ISP, the vendor can help you troubleshoot their network. The tools discussed in consideration #2 will make this process go much smoother.

Planning for an In-Office Workforce

Even with the rapid rise in remote work, many organizations continue to retain local offices for their contact centers. Having all, or many, agents located in a central location can benefit training, camaraderie, and personal accountability. But it's not without its challenges. Concentrating your resources in one location also concentrates the risk, should that location become unavailable. Here are two in-office specific considerations for the contact center.

Your Network

The fundamental purpose of a contact center, by its very name, is to make contact. Whether you choose a cloud or on-premises provider, your network eventually needs to contact the outside world. If you stay on-premises, you will work directly with various carriers to create the redundancy necessary to achieve your desired uptimes.

We will assume that since you've read this far, you're at least leaning toward — if not already on — the cloud train. In which case, focus on the question: Can your network reach the CCaaS platform?

By reach we mean all the data center and service locations comprising the CCaaS solution. For instance:

- Will you need an MPLS setup?
- If so, will the vendor provide it?
- What is the lead time?
- If your network isn't currently up to task, how long will it take you to fix it to prevent tromboning?

The lead time for a circuit is often fixed and beyond your control. But if you neglect to place an order for one early in the process because you forgot to consider the impact of single-access internet gateways, for example, that's on you. Don't set yourself up to delay an implementation by skipping this crucial step.

Multinational companies might benefit from using SD-WAN[23] instead of MPLS so you can use split tunneling to provide access to global resources. Design these and other creative networking solutions with your vendor's connectivity team early in the project so you can align the expectations of the business units with the timelines for connectivity.

Business Continuity

While we hope the "send everyone home" days of the pandemic are behind us, there are many other reasons a single location poses a risk to your business continuity.

I've seen contact centers close for floods, power outages, hurricanes, tornadoes, and someone driving a backhoe into a circuit — twice. Depending on your device policy, temporarily relocating to an alternate location or shifting to a work-from-home setup might

---

[23] A software-defined wide area network is a virtualized service that connects and extends enterprise networks over large physical distances.

be as simple as logging into the CCaaS platform from a new location. But consider these use cases when designing your network:

- Can agents access the corporate VPN if the office has no power?
- What happens if your MPLS provider has an outage?
- How many ISPs service your building?
- Do all cables enter the building through a single location that might be vulnerable (to a backhoe, for instance)?

It'd be a shame to move to a highly available cloud solution only to put a single point of failure between you and an otherwise solid business continuity plan.

Where Does the Data Flow?

In a regulatory environment where privacy, data security, and data residency requirements vary by country, it's important to understand where your customer data flows. Highly distributed cloud deployments might include components where you don't expect them.

If your data must stay in-country — or specifically remain outside of another country — make sure you understand and map the data and call flows. Your vendor's connectivity team should be happy to help you during this process. Simply bring them the results of your internal discovery thus far regarding the locations of your customers and staff.

Furthermore, be on the lookout for unexpected tromboning. Geographic proximity doesn't guarantee low latency. In South America, a voice point of presence (POP) in Brazil might imply low-latency, high-quality voice in Uruguay — they are neighbors after all. However, much to the dismay of many telecom engineers, local carriers in South America often "tie" together in Miami. (Yes, the one in Florida.)

Moral of the story: Trombones hide in unexpected places. Do your homework; make a map.

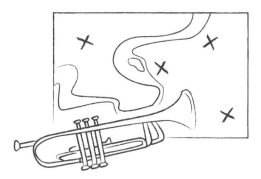

Troublesome Regions

Like I mentioned, since most countries in South America are on their own backbone, connectivity between them all route through Miami before making it to their final destination — can you hear the trombones playing yet? But that's not the only telephony headache you'll encounter when designing a multinational contact center solution.

The geopolitical situations in China, North Korea, and Russia make it difficult, if not impossible, to build and maintain infrastructure. Their respective rules regarding data residency complicate deployments, making these undesirable locations for many providers to invest in infrastructure. If you do business here, plan extra time to build out the necessary infrastructure to support your solution.

Like South America, India has isolated telecom infrastructure for domestic calling. Asia, in general, has a similar challenge; some countries don't yet support SIP[24] and run everything over copper instead (yikes!). In Egypt, the European Union, and Canada, you can expect residency or regulatory requirements that go above and beyond the typical deployment.

---

[24] Session Initiation Protocol is a signaling protocol used in Internet telephony, private IP telephone systems, and LTE mobile calling.

Other International "Gotchas"

Here's a quick list of some gotchas my clients have experienced when evaluating CCaaS providers:

- Provision of ANI[25] in global locations
- Data residency requirements for call recordings — as the final resting place for them is often not on the CCaaS platform
- The location of the AI: It's often provided by a third party like Google, IBM, or Amazon, which could affect your data's path
- Local language support for your implementation
- Day 2 support
- Language support and standardization in the user interface

In addition to strong connectivity and sales engineering services, an experienced CCaaS provider will have a compliance department ready to guide you with expertise and experience.

PROCESS PIONEERS

Owen's Expedition into International Waters

The CTO of a global logistics company, Owen is challenged with the company's lack of a centralized communication platform. Previous efforts by the head office to get the regional branches to adopt a new platform have failed. Regional IT teams cite local compliance requirements as the issue. Owen is sure that there's a vendor than can meet the needs for everyone. Sure enough, there's little resistance from regional leads when he introduces CCaaS.

---

[25] Automatic number identification refers to the number of the phone setting up the connection; while not exactly the same thing, it can help to think of the ANI as the caller ID. Whereas the DNIS (dialed number identification service) is the number you're calling.

However, they still need to ensure compliance with local regulations, especially in Egypt which has recently passed a GDPR-like regulation.

Owen: We all have those days when we wake up and just don't want to go to work. The mere thought of the day's tasks makes you want to go back to bed, roll up in the duvet, and wake up on a tropical island.

For me, those days came toward the end of every month. I'm one of those annoying, overly jovial morning people. But the last week of the month was when I had to review the performance reports from the contact centers for all our regional branches to identify areas needing improvement. I hated it with a passion. It wasn't because I don't love my job; it was because I knew there had to be a better way to do it than manually scrolling through spreadsheets.

The problem was that we used different contact center platforms in various branches, so we lacked a centralized place to manage all the data. If we'd had a single platform across our branches, it would have been easy to pull the data in real time to find useful performance insights.

Unfortunately, the regional IT heads balked every time I brought up the subject. Their reasoning was that they needed to uphold local laws and compliance standards, which meant they were best served by a local vendor with local data centers. I couldn't argue against that. What was a little manual work if it helped save the company from potential lawsuits and a damaged reputation?

When I look back, I suspect it was more that the regional leads didn't like the idea of a suit in the head office telling them how to run things in their own yard. But guess who had the last laugh? Me. I found the perfect solution that they couldn't reject. (We all had the last laugh because the software ended up being mutually beneficial and completely transformed our contact center.)

All the other solutions I had explored always seemed to be missing a critical feature. If it wasn't compliance, then it was something like limited integration. CCaaS ticked all the boxes.

It was exactly what I had been looking for. To begin with, it has SOC 2 Type 2 attestation, which means it has all the right security controls to ensure data protection and conform with regulators with controls like firewalls, intrusion detection systems, and full-time security staff. Moreover, our vendor had data centers around the globe, which addresses the low-latency issue.

The other critical selling point for regions is we can use our own telephony services. This is perfect for areas where local carriers provide reliable services at a lower cost than partner carriers.

We also have an easy way to build and manage IVAs. With our previous solution, we had to rely on outside development resources, which cost us time and money.

Armed with this information, I called for an interregional meeting. And since I was going in to win, I made sure we had a vendor rep present.

Today is the last day of the month and, for the first time in years, I don't feel like I need a two-day retreat to a Caribbean island to cool my mind. Ironically, I now do performance reviews twice a month. But with a centralized contact center platform, I enjoy doing it.

We're still working on how to implement the solution in Egypt because of a new data privacy regulation. The provisions outline how the data of Egypt's citizens should be processed and limits the transfer of citizen data outside the country without consent. I'm working on a meeting with a compliance expert in the region to discuss how we can deploy the new solution while ensuring we stay compliant.

Choosing Channels

Once upon a time, voice was the undisputed royalty of the contact center. A recent consumer preferences survey[26] found customers' affinity for voice decreased by 9% to 51%, while their inclination for digital increased by 26% to 43% compared to one year prior. That's a big shift. And it's accelerating. Voice may still be leading, but no longer overwhelmingly.

You need a well-planned strategy for digital channels to avoid the risk of alienating your customers. To unpack the best ways to incorporate digital into your overall customer communications strategy and balance it with voice (which is undergoing a bit of a digital revolution itself), let's look at three big shifts underway in the market.

"Digital First"

Think about the last time you wanted to invite a friend to dinner. Not someone with whom you have romantic interest, just a friend from school or work. Pretend you're visiting their town and thought it'd be fun to grab a bite.

Now, did you call them? Or send them a text?

If you're anything like me, this imagined scenario takes place in the middle of the workday — around the time you received the green light to book the trip. To avoid forgetting about it, you decide to ask them right then. Except... it's the middle of the workday and you haven't spoken to this person in a few weeks, so a phone call might send the wrong message. We'd hate to have them confuse our urgent need (to remember the task) with an emergent situation necessitating a live call and immediate attention. So, you shoot them a text.

---

[26] "Five9 Customer Service Index 2021," Five9. https://www.five9.com/resources/report-five9-customer-service-index-2021

Whatever that message reads, the point is the same — you went digital first. Even my mom texts me before she calls now. (I never asked her to, for the record.) She just prefers to coordinate a good social gathering using a nondisruptive communication channel.

As more people adopt a digital-first lifestyle, the expectation of what's considered normal or acceptable ways of contact will follow. In the not-so-distant future, I expect it to become (even more) rude for a business to call a customer without texting first. On the flip side, customers will expect to be able to send your business a message without being forced into the voice channel. Just like we could finalize lunch plans with or without speaking live, customers expect similar options.

Imagine a world where customers can message you on the channel they find most convenient, go as far through the journey as suits them, and then change channels on a dime. Because like you — who might have gone up and back a few times about lunch spots before you decided it'd be faster to discuss it live — your customers expect the conversation context to carry through to the live call. Digital first. Audio, optionally. No repeats. That's the expectation.

> DIGITAL FIRST. AUDIO, OPTIONALLY. NO REPEATS. THAT'S THE EXPECTATION.

Even when a customer calls your organization before messaging you, they expect a digital experience. No one expects a live person to answer when calling a business of any size. Years of bad IVRs have conditioned people to expect they'll be greeted by an automated experience. Here's your opportunity to sidestep their premeditated disappointment and deliver a digital (audio) experience that delights.

A Glimpse into the Future

Imagine using a digital assistant to set up your lunch. Whether you call or message, you state your intention: "I want to grab sushi with Sam next time I'm in Vegas." And the AI takes it from there.

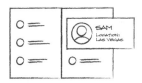

1. It cross-references your address book to identify which Sam lives in Vegas

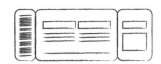

2. Checks your email for flight confirmations to sort out when you'll be there

3. Accesses Sam's public calendar and reconciles their availability with yours

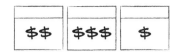

4. Retrieves your preferences for moderately priced restaurants based on its analysis of your previous purchase history

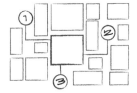

5. Sees that Sam's office is located near three sushi restaurants

6. Confirms a reservation at the option with the quietest vibe according to online reviews so you can enjoy the conversation

Wouldn't that be amazing?!? Having a virtual assistant understand all the nuance and steps involved in the process of "going to lunch" and execute on a plan without my intervention. That would change my life for sure.

How close are we to making this a reality in business? Closer than you might think. Substitute any business-related scheduling — like a medical appointment or financial planning meeting

— and you can see. With a few changes, clever database dips, and the help of solid customer profiling, we can proactively retrieve the data and takes the steps to create very impressive digital-first experiences.

The Rise of Messaging

An increased preference for and prevalence of digital messaging channels — web chat, SMS/text, and social platforms — is also driving change. Of the 40% of companies that added a new channel in 2022, 53% turned to messaging — apps like WhatsApp, texting, and messaging embedded in a company's own website — according to a Zendesk[27] study.

Demographic changes appear to drive this trend as more tech-savvy customers enjoy the convenience and ease of using messaging vs. voice and other channels, like email. In addition to demographic influences on modality, consider the cultural norms and preferences of regional customer populations. The study uncovered an interesting geographic tilt, with SMS/text being more popular in North America while WhatsApp dominates in other geographies. I expect as social media messaging platforms come and go, similar fluctuations in regional preferences will emerge.

Omnichannel, for Real

The term omnichannel has lost its meaning due to mis- and inconsistent use. The original spirit of the idea was cool: The notion of using any channel to communicate, whichever is most convenient, and the promise of switching between them seamlessly certainly appeals to me. Yet in practice, I seem to be the only one who thinks responding to an email with an instant message is a good idea (evidenced by the fact that "huh?" is the most frequent response I receive). But I realize the reason I'm confusing my

---

[27] Customer Experience Trends 2021, Zendesk. https://www.zendesk.com/customer-experience-trends-2021/#get-the-report

friends has nothing to do with the bad — yet incredibly timely — jokes I send.

Context. Context is the issue and it's lost during the channel change.

People, even our friends, can lose the thread when you switch channels on them. Yet the channel switcher, me in this case, has a firm grasp on the thread — and expects you to keep up. Your customers don't care that different contact centers work on email vs. messaging. They expect that when they receive an email response they don't appreciate, they can start a chat to find resolution NOW.

In a real omnichannel environment — one where we return to the spirit of the term — we can achieve this level of seamless channel switching. One in which a conversation can start over email, elevate to chat, pivot to voice, finish via SMS, and thread perfectly into a video or mixed-modality IVA experience, even days or weeks later.

To ensure your contact center finds itself on the right path, look for solutions that make channel switching seamless. Solutions with which people can move from text-based interactions to voice without losing context. And where you can have multiple modalities (like audio and visual) active simultaneously — because sometimes you need more than one to accomplish your service goals.

Imagine you're in the store and can't decide if you've found the kind of melon your partner wanted, so you text them a picture while on a phone call. The same can happen in business. What if your digital assistant needs to capture an image or voiceprint, or send you options from which to choose? A real omnichannel (multimodal) experience, isn't limited by the mode on which the interaction begins. It uses the best tool for the job and delivers a truly engaging experience.

Hidden Customer Preferences

"Just because I'm standing here doesn't mean I'm happy about it."

We mistake customer actions with preferences all the time! I can't even count the number of times someone has shared survey results, to a multiple choice question, where they say: "The survey says people want blue widgets; we need to make widgets in blue." Urg! Just because people select blue over red or yellow, doesn't mean they want blue. It may just mean they dislike blue the least of the three. If you really want to know what people think about color, you need be direct and just ask: "What's your favorite widget color?"

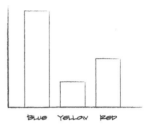

But businesses don't want to do that. Open-ended questions take longer to parse. Someone would need to read and categorize the results, and no one has time for that. Sometimes we're just too lazy — er, I mean "busy" — to survey in the first place, so we opt to infer preference based on prior action. That's even worse.

Just because customers call your contact center doesn't mean they prefer to use the phone. Similarly with written communication, if the only "contact us" button leads to a chat or email experience, your customers have no choice. In those situations, their preference is neither known nor relevant. Like zoo patrons stuck in a thunderstorm, your customers' channel selection may simply reflect a proximity to the only channel available to shelter them from the rain.

"OUR CUTOMERS LOVE HORSES!"

How Channel Choices Impact IT

Channel choice clearly impacts a cross-functional team. If you add a new phone number, someone needs to post it on the website, for example. But implementing more sophisticated digital channels will require integrations to Google Analytics, go behind authentication, or otherwise tie into existing systems.

IT should help facilitate these cross-departmental conversations to ensure key integration requirements don't get lost in translation. Even simple implementations where you "just drop a few lines of code on the website" might impact downstream functionality or would be better suited behind the customer portal than on the main .com site.

Use your extensive knowledge of all the systems available inside the business to advise the contact center on:

- How best to proceed
- Alternative middleware options (as relevant)
- Areas of the business their choice impacts
- Better ways to accomplish the task (even good ideas benefit from a fresh set of tech-savvy eyes)

One last thought on email. Many contact center solutions rely on you to bring you own mail server. If you decide to add email as a channel, the load on your email server might skyrocket overnight if your customers adopt it. It can be difficult to accurately measure pent-up demand for a previously unoffered channel. (Some customers will stubbornly stand in the rain rather than visit a horse they don't like.)

PROCESS PIONEERS

Paula Blows Up the Contact Center with Chat

Paula is a senior manager in IT operations and former head of inside sales for a global 3D printer manufacturer. She has been at the company for a little over five years and has many roles inside this burgeoning business. Recently Paula has seen their growth strain their on-premises call center.

Paula: My company handles rapid prototyping and direct digital manufacturing solutions for our clients. It sounds very fancy. Handling customer service, especially at our scale, can be very intimidating when your customers are among the global leaders in aerospace, automotive, medical, industrial, educational, and tech.

As 3D printing took off worldwide, we continued to maintain one contact center per country, some often covering multiple countries. With my background in the agriculture sector, it was funny that our company — a technology leader — had a more outdated phone system than a "bunch of farmers," as my coworkers jokingly refer to my old sales team.

Our customers and resellers call our Minnesota-based US contact for technical support. The goal is for agents to resolve 50% of incoming calls before dispatching technicians onsite. Goal is the key word here; our numbers were closer to 20% or 30%.

Inside sales, order management, support, logistics, and accounts payable were all part of the contact center. It was a mess. We tried implementing menu options and hiring additional agents, but we couldn't "press 1 or 2" ourselves out of this. We even added a chat feature on our website so clients could reach agents without having to wait on hold for hours. We had no idea that there were thousands of customers just waiting to chat. It made things worse!

It turns out that waiting for a return text is more frustrating than waiting on the phone. We often found ourselves the target of what I like to call the "all-caps avalanche." A customer, tired of waiting, would just start yelling!

Unfortunately, without a more efficient way to handle all these calls or automate the chats, we knew the screaming would continue. It was crushing to see agents breaking down, feeling like they were set up to fail. At the same time, I became resentful of our customers and felt like they weren't giving us a fair shot to service them.

I do get the customer perspective. It's not OK to spend a significant amount of money on a product and then not receive the support you need to operate. I knew I was putting our sales team in a tough place. It became more difficult for them to guarantee a certain level of service without feeling like frauds. I had sales agents threaten to quit, and the internal tension between our teams grew. But, again, we knew that the contact center wasn't at fault. It just didn't have the tools to succeed. I needed to step up.

When we implemented, it was like night and day. Suddenly, our agents had access to our Salesforce CRM and could log calls more reliably. We realized there's a more innovative way to incorporate chat on our website and that our old setup made things worse.

My team helped the business units discover that a vast percentage of customers were simply asking for documentation that was easy to find online. We implemented an interactive visual menu to give customers another route to communicate. It guides customers through options to find documentation, email for support within 24 hours, or submit a request form to have the next available agent contact them.

And get this: Our agent calls them!

The call experience has also greatly improved. As a customer calls in, the Salesforce integration allows agents to see their previous interactions via screen pops. Armed with the history, agents can make customers feel more understood and get to the reason they called faster. Meanwhile, the team morale has improved significantly. The "all-caps avalanches" are in the past and the team dives headfirst into every morning. I couldn't have asked for more!

Forecasting Capacity and Need

Those with an established contact center might feel they have a solid handle on their capacity and the flow of incoming inquiries, but — as they say in the stock market — past performance does not guarantee future results.

What happens when a video of your product goes viral on social media and the phones ring off the hook? Will marketing be okay with a "well, we didn't expect that many calls" response? What if a surprise severe weather incident impacts your customer base? Will you have the capacity to help? Or will a busy signal, signal to your customers that you're too busy for them?

Build the House for Birthday Parties?

With cloud, adding more lines can be as simple as reaching out to your account manager or accessing an online provisioning portal.

But for on-premises applications, you have to decide: Should we build a house big enough to accommodate Grandma's 90th birthday blowout, five years from now? Or would it be easier and more cost-effective to just rent a tent that day? I mean: We want to believe Grandma will live that long (that our company will grow over time, or that a killer marketing campaign will yield sudden burst in demand) but it's a risk. Shall we spend a lot now, or come up with temporary "tent" solution later?

Even those on "team tent" — often represented by a business process outsourcer (BPO) or otherwise separate team or application — know it comes with some tradeoffs. For one, the people in the tent seldom have the same experience as those who get to party in the house. If you're a brand that values the experience you provide, it might prove difficult to choose which guests sit outside while the rest are comfortable indoors.

Have you ever had that dream where you discover hidden rooms in your house? (Just me?) Well, choosing a cloud solution is like living in a magic house with hidden rooms just in case you need them one day. So, when Grandma turns 90 — and she totally will; she's super spry — your house can magically expand to host 90 years of friends and family.

How Volumes Vary by Channel

Forecasting agent requirements can get complicated since you can handle some interactions simultaneously while others need a more asynchronous approach. Your business partners don't only need to think about how many lines or active chat ports they need to address customer demand. They also need to consider the number of agents they'll need. And it's not linear math.

Synchronicity of Interactions

Think of interactions as belonging to three categories:

- Synchronous (real time) interactions, like voice, require active engagement and low latency.
- Semi-synchronous, like messaging, are still active conversations, but may not require the same level of constant attention as voice.
- Asynchronous interactions, like email, carry little expectation of an immediate response.

Messaging sits in a bit of a gray area. What does semi-synchronous mean anyway? To better understand where an interaction falls along the synchronous-asynchronous spectrum, consider the following exercise.

Pretend you're on the phone with your partner. You ask them a question. Now, how long of a delay would you accept before accusing them of multitasking, having a bad connection, or otherwise not listening to you? Not long, right? Certainly not long enough for them to carry on a separate, simultaneous conversation. Voice is, therefore, synchronous.

Now pretend you send them a text. Do you expect an immediate response? Maybe not. But once they do respond, are you a bit annoyed when a conversation doesn't flow? Like if they respond and you immediately reply, but then they wait like 10 minutes to respond again... Are you super understanding or do you think: "You just had your phone in your hand! What happened?"

So, parts are asynchronous: You're OK with the initiation of the conversation being non-immediate, but less OK with pronounced delays for the ongoing bits of the interaction.

Then there's chat. With chat, I personally expect a more immediate initial response. And I've become conditioned by the contact center industry to accept a multitasking-induced delay between subsequent exchanges. I don't love it, but I expect it. So, both SMS and chat are semi-synchronous, albeit with different customer expectations.

Your business partners in the contact center need to provide you a baseline of customer expectations — such as how much delay they will tolerate — so you can help them estimate how agents should handle simultaneous interactions. But they might not know.

Most contact centers focus solely on a response-time service-level agreement (SLA[28]) of how long the customer initially waited. Lend a consulting hand by helping them understand how multitasking can impact another critical measure: customer satisfaction, and suggest they experiment to find the sweet spot between effective scale through agent multitasking and customer frustration. The number of simultaneous actions that fit in the sweet spot will vary from agent to agent: Some people just juggle better than others. So, make sure you choose a solution that can handle this level of granular optimization.

For those of you looking for a place to start the math, agents can typically handle:

- 3 to 5 simultaneous chats
- 10 emails at a time
- 1 voice or video conversation

---

[28] Service level agreements are a way to contractually promise system availability or support response time and designate any negotiated penalties for failure to deliver in advance.

Concurrency of Interactions

From IT's perspective, when it comes to right-sizing the infrastructure, you need to ensure you have enough ports for voice traffic and are licensed to handle sufficient concurrent sessions for the digital interactions. Your customers will receive a busy signal if your phone system lacks available lines (voice ports). Rude, but less tragic than the chat equivalent: a "connection refused" message. Port availability is also important inside the self-service channels. Virtual assistants might have components that require a port of their own, but only for small sections of the interaction — for example during speech recognition.

Hopefully, you have sufficient historical data from your existing platform to estimate concurrent interactions you can expect on a new system. But if not, or you're not confident that there isn't a litany of unserviced interactions lurking — for example, people who got busy signals without you knowing — then ask your contact center vendor for help. Especially when it comes to sizing self-service applications like IVAs, they have the expertise and insights to help ensure you purchase enough lines. And if you don't, no big deal. That's why you're in the cloud. You can always scale up and move into one of those secret rooms in the house. ;)

PROCESS PIONEERS

Louise Rocks the Guesswork

Louise works for a national florist chain specializing in online ordering with local shops fulfilling the orders. She has grown with the company, starting when it served just one state to where it is now, supporting all 48 continental states. Typical seasonal forecasting models don't always work for the floral industry. Louise was desperate to find a solution that could help her team better predict customer swells for staffing and training purposes.

Louise: I started out very young in this industry. I worked in my uncle's flower shop during my high-school summers. I thought I would live and die in the family business, but life had other plans. I fell in love with computer science during college and found myself on the path to a career in IT. So, after graduation, I was delighted to find a job as an IT specialist at a retail floral startup in my home state of Texas that was starting to gain momentum and expand beyond that region. I knew the company had lofty goals to become a national brand. With my work and family history, I felt I could be an invaluable resource.

Although I knew flowers, I knew little about startups and business. I thought the internal clock I had developed over years of working with my uncle would be enough to handle any forecasting to manage workload. It turns out, seasonal demands vary from region to region!

I was fortunate that, early on in our expansion, we decided to use workforce automation and customer data integration. After just one year, we could forecast much more efficiently for the following year and be prepared for any increase in demand. Industries like ours often have surges where we will need 50x as many workers and 200x as many lines seemingly overnight.

It's never actually overnight — if you know what to look for. We just need to be able to accurately assess the previous year's data to forecast for people and capacity so we can hire and train the necessary team.

For example, wedding season is an easy guess for a busy time for any floral retailer. Growing up in Texas, however, Easter and Christmas far outweighed wedding season in terms of floral sales. But in New York, Mother's Day is the busiest flower day of the year, while the rest of wedding season is relatively light. You'd never believe it if you didn't have the numbers in front of you, but now we do.

In our first year with the new system, I scaled up my team leading into November, convinced that we would be slammed for the holidays. I hadn't considered that we had recently opened service to the entire Northeast United States. I was applying my numbers from one region to our entire company, and it caused an embarrassing amount of waste in our first year. (I needed to scale, but not that much!) What's worse, we had to extend many of the short-term temp workers to cover the actual busy season, which dipped into the reserve budgets we hadn't allocated for the first quarter.

The following year, I was ready. Workforce optimization (WFO) made it easy to draw insights about trends in call volumes and customer preferences; it seemed to understand and recognize all the floral-specific terms. I couldn't believe that the reports came from a piece of software! Imagine seeing forecasts broken down by every imaginable demographic and region.

Next, we implemented chat, which let us broaden engagement and reduce the need to add staff during peak seasons since agents could service multiple customers at once. Also, while most of our agents were in Texas, moving to the cloud has broadened our geographic talent pool. It is easy to scale quickly now. And we can automatically prioritize leads from multiple sources and auto-route them to preferred call lists or agents. Intelligent routing helps maximize performance by routing calls to the agents with the highest ratings.

Without these cost-saving measures, we couldn't have expanded as quickly as we did. Off the top, we realized 15% to 20% savings in technology and telecommunications costs. And being able to walk into any strategy meeting with the data we have from the system has allowed us to announce our first international expansion into Canada at the end of next year.

It's cool thinking about that girl from a small Texas town who now leads the IT department of a soon-to-be international retailer.

Don't Get in Your Own Way

A large retailer chose to build its own automatic call distributor (ACD)[29]. The bespoke build allowed the retailer to use agent availability data to dynamically add, remove, or change phone numbers posted on its site based on a customer's eligibility to make a call.

(So yeah, all those times you thought you were seeing things — the number was totally there yesterday but no one else saw it — it might be the business dynamically determining your eligibility for support and obfuscating the phone numbers accordingly. This is such a neat idea.)

The only issue was that the retailer came to my team with a predetermined notion of how to solve the problem in the context of our solution. IT wanted real-time agent status so it could make the decisions like it always has. But since IT didn't include anyone on the business side to provide input, we couldn't explore alternative ways to:

- Not overwhelm the contact center
- Provide support to all eligible customers

While we ultimately sorted it out, the experience was more painful than necessary. I can't stress enough the importance of including the business decision makers in the conversation early and often.

---

[29] The automatic call distributer is the "brain" of the contact center that decides where and to whom to route a call.

> IT'S EASY TO GET TECHIE
> TUNNEL VISION; YOUR
> BUSINESS COUNTERPARTS
> CAN OFFER A WIDER VIEW.

PROCESS PIONEERS

How Skyler Scaled

Skyler is a new dad who works in IT at a quickly growing university. With enrollment doubling within the last five years, his team needed all the help they could get with scaling so all its employees and prospective students could succeed.

Skyler: It's amazing how much your views on working in higher education shift when you have a kid. When my husband and I adopted our son, I knew I wanted to give him the world. However, I didn't expect those emotions around my own family to spill over into my work. I saw all these kids venturing into the world for the first time and I wanted to ensure that I was part of setting them up for success.

Our university has provided online education since 1999. My department oversees IT for the contact center, primarily focusing on outbound calls for admissions, financial aid, and student advisory services. I started here more than 10 years ago when our contact center was an on-premises solution installed more than 10 years earlier.

IT is responsible for running the contact center, which employs 300 agents who handle more than 40,000 calls per week. When I started, they managed about 10,000 a week. In the early 2000s, we started pushing more people to our website to try to reduce stress on our agents. But our solution had prospective students complete an online form — and our agents were expected to call them within two to five seconds of receiving the form. Not only did it not reduce call volumes, but we didn't have web-to-campaign automation, so the team had to manually, frantically call people to meet the SLA.

It was just one of those things that often happens, especially in higher education, where you keep slapping Band-Aids on problems until you eventually step back and realize you've created a weird mutant mummy made entirely of bandages! Fortunately, we completely overhauled our IT systems with grant money from the state.

Faced with rapid growth, we migrated from an on-premises solution to a CCaaS platform. The university leadership was eager to switch so it could set larger growth goals. We'd need the ability to make more calls and respond faster to online inquiries. Our on-prem solution was incapable of scaling and integrating. Cloud was the only logical choice. Using automation, we doubled call volume without increasing staff.

Implementation was initially a bit difficult, but some of that was messaging failures on our end. People can be wary of new tech. And you can expect resistance when you have a staff that has used the same system for more than a decade. We put several agents on the new system for a couple of weeks during testing. About half hated it at first and swore it would never work. I remember begging people to give it a chance, put in the time, and they'd see the benefits.

When I went back to those same people two weeks later, they were hooked! I thanked them for being early adopters and asked them to go back to the old system until the official full-company go-live. Several of them refused.

Over the years, it's been exciting to see the average age of our students shift: It used to be 42, it's now 33. When we began, we primarily targeted older generations who were returning to school or making a career change. In the past decade, we've seen a massive boom in online education attracting kids just out of high school or looking to take classes prior to graduating. Our students want to connect with us in different ways, so we need to scale across many communication platforms. Some want to use the phone, but the more internet-savvy prefer chat or email. We now have much greater flexibility to meet those ever-changing needs and scale depending on the incoming student population each year.

Engaging students and ensuring they feel cared for is important to me. When my son goes to college, I want him to have easy access to the people guiding his education. I never want him to feel like a number. With our university population spread across the country, it can be easy to slip into that feeling.

When an agent receives an inbound call, a screen pop provides the caller's student profile. The agent sees all the data and interaction history, which allows them to personalize a contextual experience. Our students don't have to repeat their stories every time they call.

I guarantee we have a better communications system than some of the top universities. It never gets in our way and always scales to meet our needs. With the technology out of the way, I know the sky's the limit. We have just scratched the surface of the quality of education and related support services we can deliver.

CHAPTER SIX

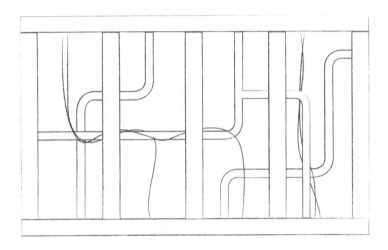

ROUGHING IN THE PIPES AND OUTLETS

Now that we know the size of our new home and who will occupy each room, we're ready to install the plumbing and electrical. That is, it's time to get specific about the integration requirements. Where do we need sinks, toilets, and tubs? Where, specifically, will we have to plug in to other applications? Because we should definitely place an outlet there.

We need to consider how our contact center staff will utilize the space, day to day. Consider:

- What business applications do they need on their desktops?
- Who else helps agents get things done?
- How often does your company add/change software vendors?

This knowledge will equip you to choose a solution that doesn't force you to run extension cords all over the place. You'll have outlets where you need them.

CRM: Customer Relationship Management

For the purposes of this book, CRM generically refers to your contact center's primary system of record. Internally you may refer to it as an electronic medical record (EMR), ticketing system, customer database, or Dianne — like one of my more entertaining customers.

In this context, the specific utility of the tool is less important than its role in enabling your team to interact successfully with clients or customers.

(By the way... if you haven't selected cloud by now, life is about to become more painful than necessary.)

Let the System(s) of Record Be the System(s) of Record

Your contact center dream home should support an easy, deep integration with your CRM tool. We discussed data residency concerns earlier in the "Identifying Impacted Geographies" chapter, and one way to simplify the compliance requirements of your solution is to not copy data from multiple systems of record into your contact center application for no reason. Modern CCaaS platforms offer deep integrations between their platform, the user experience, and the CRM application(s).

Think of your contact center solution as a — likely AI-powered — logistics engine. It knows where you house all important information, what data to access, how to interpret the particulars for routing, when your team needs help, and where to put the results. Just like Google doesn't need to be the internet to know the internet, your CCaaS platform doesn't need to be a system of record for it to enable your team to reach their goals.

Can it? Sure. But why? Your business units have likely already selected a best-of-breed, cloud CRM–like solution to power their parts of the business. So, let's enhance the value of those solutions by making it super easy to deliver more engaging customer and employee experiences.

Your chosen solution should satisfy current functionality — usually something simple like a screen pop — and offer capabilities to curate content from multiple systems of record into a streamlined employee experience. Look for capabilities like productized adapters for your CRM, easy API-level[30] integrations to popular CRM vendors, and automatic call memorialization (interaction logging).

What If We Change Vendors?

Your contact center solution should accommodate whatever CRM vendor you choose, even if you change your mind or switch vendors in the future. It should simplify that transition by providing consistency for your agents during the transition. Switching CRM vendors is complex and requires a ton of work to map and clean data, etc., but your contact center vendor shouldn't make it worse, and shouldn't be a showstopper. Any vendor says it can't help you with such a change doesn't have enough hands-on experience of practical contact center technology.

Be leery of any vendor that integrates with only one or two CRM applications. Avoid solutions that don't function without a CRM: What happens when the CRM has an outage? Will that bring down your contact center too? It shouldn't! You'll want a solution that offers value independently of your data source(s) while making it drop-dead easy to capitalize on the value locked within them.

Multiple CRMs, Single Contact Center

Accommodate multiple CRMs. Full stop. This use case is so common that even if your entire company standardizes on a single platform, I'd still recommend you choose a vendor that can

---

[30] Application programming interfaces are the way two software applications speak to each other or share data.

simultaneously support multiple CRMs. You never know what a rogue line of business owner will get approval to do next. In fact, there are plenty of strong reasons to require an application to have integration options for multiple CRMs.

Remember we're using CRM colloquially to mean the software that manages your customer relationship. Imagine you're a pharmaceutical company with multiple contact centers:

- One department might speak to consumers directly. In this case your "customer" is the person taking the medication and your CRM is an EMR database.
- A sales department interacts with referring doctors and uses a more traditional salesforce automation-type CRM to keep track of their deals.
- Your IT department's customers are your organization's employees for which the CRM is a ticketing system for managing cases.
- Human resources might use a specialized CRM for employee records, benefit management, and so on.

Four departments, four applications. Would you recommend or expect your HR department to use a medical records system? Of course not. So don't accept a contact center application without native support for multiple integrations.

Our CRM Game Is Chaotic

In the previous example, the company had a clean set of CRMs. Most companies don't. Organizations that have been around for a while have a fair amount of technical messiness. Fear not. Database chaos shouldn't stop a modern contact center platform. If anything, it should help tame the turmoil.

If it takes a dip into 14 databases to collect all the data necessary to deliver an excellent customer and agent experience, so be it. We're out to build our contact center forever home, right? Don't let the pain you've experienced in the past stifle your dreams.

An agent doesn't need to know that the data they receive in the contact center application comes from lots of little truths scattered throughout your CRM neighborhood. They only need to worry about having what they need to carry on the customer conversation and their notes end up where they belong. If your contact center application can do that, you're off to a good start.

The Chicken and the Egg

Given the close tie between a contact center's value and the CRM application, you might wonder if you need to choose one before the other. Of course not. Does it help? Sure. But it's not mandatory.

I once worked with a company that used a completely closed, on-premises CRM with no API capabilities whatsoever. Technically they had a CRM, but for the purposes of the contact center project, it might as well have not existed because we couldn't access its data.

Many of the efficiency gains you'd expect from use cases like screen pop and automatically greeting a customer by name weren't a given like they were for many other clients. But that doesn't mean the CCaaS solution didn't add value. It added tons of value! We just had to get creative. In the end, the business benefited from its limited CRM approach because it allowed them to take a first principles approach to rethinking their customer's experience.

If you're on the verge of implementing a new CRM — or one for the first time — it can make sense to do it before changing your contact center solution. Knowing your future data model up front can save you from having to reimplement the contact center solution unnecessarily. On the flip side, if you proceed with the CCaaS solution first, don't make the mistake of integrating the old, on-its-way-out CRM into the new system in the meantime. It will just introduce bad habits and unnecessary technical debt into your new solution. If that thought even crosses your mind, it's best thing to wait and implement both at the same time.

Do it once; do it well.

UC: Unified Communications

Unified communications does NOT equal contact center! In fact, run the other way if your UC partner tries to sell you a contact center. The contact center is an attractive expansion area for UC vendors and partners because contact center margins are typically better, way better. And no, that does not mean you should ask for a bigger discount. But it does beg the question: Why have margins compressed so much in the UC space?

Margins have compressed because UC platforms typically don't add much sophistication. They add value, sure: Everyone needs a way to communicate with colleagues, coworkers, and customers. But they don't need incredibly sophisticated ways of doing so.

Contact center solutions, on the other hand, come with a myriad of sophisticated routing, enablement, and "smart" features that allow you to deliver value to those arms of the organization in ways simple dial-tone and collaboration-focused products cannot.

To distinguish between UC and contact center use cases, return to the technique we used earlier in the book. Ask yourself: Does the person calling in need to speak to Jane specifically, or just someone with Jane's skill set and expertise? When it's specifically Jane, we're talking UC; if it's someone like Jane, we should land in the contact center.

But the line is blurring. Another way to evaluate audience is to ask how many hours a day Jane "should" engage with customers. If a person's job is to interact with customers for more than half of the workday, it's likely that a contact center solution will benefit them. More than 60% and they definitely need a contact center license.

What If We're Only a Call Center?

If you're providing only phone support, you might think you can get away with using less-sophisticated features that typically accompany a UC vendor–provided "contact center" solution.

In the short term, you're probably correct. But ask yourself:

- Where will my business be in five years?
- Where will our customers be?
- Does the vendor's roadmap match where we're going?
- What will we risk if we must wait for features?
- Do we want to always be a beta customer, first to utilize the vendor's latest functionality?

The answers may lead you to realize that the shift to omnichannel customer experiences is already happening. Which, frankly, shouldn't come as a surprise. As Gen Z ages into the economy, bringing their text-before-you-call tendencies, the channel of first touch will continue to evolve. This will put even more pressure on the business to have interactions flow between channels and teams smoothly because not every issue can (or should) be solved over instant message.

Sure, being on the bleeding edge can be exciting, but boring still works. Don't worry, the voice channel won't disappear completely. It will always be the best way to communicate tone and complex, emotional ideas.

As you evolve from call center to contact center, you'll want a partner with experience. Choosing a vendor focused entirely on contact center will save you the hassle of being the customer that teaches them the lessons. They've been there, done that — and can now guide you.

All philosophical rantings aside — your business will likely need both solutions. If you don't want two vendors, hire for the harder use case, and find a contact center solution that sells UC (instead of the other way around).

How UC and CC Should Integrate

Unlike CRM where two-way integrations are crucial, a one-way integration will usually suffice for contact center and UC. Because, typically, an agent will need someone specific from the back office to help on a client call, but not the reverse.

For example, imagine a customer calls to check on the status of a refund. The agent sees the refund has been processed, but the customer has not received a payment, so they conference with someone from accounting to sort out the discrepancy. The contact center agent needs visibility into who is available in accounting so they can quickly select — by themselves — the best person to connect with.

The reverse is much less common. Should an office worker require the help of a contact center agent, they'd be best off just calling the center themselves. Calls routed to agents inside the contact center are distributed automatically. There's an algorithm. There's automation. If they're in a meeting, the system ensures you get the next "best" agent already — no need for humans to gum up the works. Furthermore, agents set themselves "unavailable" before stepping away to ensure no interactions mistakenly land on their desktop. There's no need for a secondary representation of their availability like that in a UC platform because the contact center platform already has it handled.

Look for a contact center solution that offers an integration with your UC provider that:

- Shows agents the real-time availability of back-office users
- Supports conferencing and transferring of calls originating in the contact center
- Accommodates call recording and memorialization requirements

Food for Thought: Forecasting Need

When you simplify something, more people will do it. Collaboration between the contact center and back office is no exception. Take the time to consider the impact easier access will have on the productivity of your back-office users. Thinking back to the refund example, can you imagine the level of disruption they'd experience if every accountant in finance suddenly received 50 calls a day from the contact center?

Most contact center solution providers will, at some point during the engagement, discuss workforce management. With those solutions come features that automate forecasting, scheduling, and shift management. They've optimized these solutions to accommodate the variable nature of omnichannel and shift work in a contact center. Only recently, however, have vendors begun discussing how to measure, forecast, and plan for the impact enhanced collaboration has on back-office workers.

While technology and best practices in this area are still emerging, it's a discussion you should absolutely start inside your organization. Not only will it help you solidify yourself as that trusted advisor/in-house consultant, but it will also help the business hedge against the negative impacts of easy collaboration.

Simply putting a "rules of engagement" plan in place as you roll out new functionality to the contact center can mitigate an otherwise detrimental influx of calls. Also set up a formalized feedback loop so the affected business users can share their experiences and offer suggestions for internal process improvements.

It's yet another way IT can bring people together.

Regional Parity

Cloud-to-cloud integrations are generally pretty straightforward, so connecting your UC as a service (UCaaS[31]) solution to your cloud contact center (or CCaaS[32]) solution shouldn't require too much thought. But if you have a multinational or otherwise geographically segmented deployment — or you're connecting your new CCaaS solution to an on-premises or hosted UC solution — pay special attention to the location of the data centers.

---

[31] Unified communications as a service, a more common way to refer to cloud UC providers.

[32] Contact center as a service is the colloquial term for "cloud" contact center platforms.

Because when calling Ulysses the UC user, the caller expects to reach either Ulysses or his voicemail. It doesn't matter if Ulysses's phone is in the same regional deployment as another employee. Consequently, some UC deployments are very compartmentalized. This shouldn't represent an unsurmountable challenge for integration; it's just something to consider during the design phase of your implementation. Compartmentalization can be good: It can simplify the number of departments to which the contact center has access. Agents probably don't need to conference with HR on an outbound sales call, for example.

The Importance of Flexibility and Vendor Agnosticism

UC solutions are a commodity. Many vendors do it well (and several don't). Due to the ease of installation, UCaaS isn't the high consideration purchase it once was. It's easier than ever to change providers. If your vendor suddenly experiences quality or reliability issues, you can swap to another one. If you expand into an unsupported region, you might add a second provider to cover it. Whatever the reason for the change, you don't want to tie the hands of one aspect of your business based on decisions made by another.

That's the value IT can add: Empower each area of the organization to maintain autonomy. Like a mother who lets her child stir the pot, she will stop them from touching the boiling soup. But if all hands remain firmly on the spoon, Mom lets the munchkins do it by themselves. So, help your organization select a vendor that preserves future options with a solution that integrates easily with a variety of UC providers.

Efrain Engages the Back Office

Efrain works as an IT manager for a large online retailer. His workplace recently decided to commit to overhauling its on-premises contact centers and bring them into the fully digital world. Efrain's push to truly unify the retailer's total communication solutions has allowed it to grow while giving his IT department a full range of support to handle any scaling.

Efrain: In early 2021, our company committed to migrate to a digital, cloud contact center, allowing our sales and customer service teams to work remotely. When we started, I could tell that the focus would be prioritizing agent-customer communications. But we weren't preparing for any internal communications beyond the systems we already had in place.

My work motto is "there is no such thing as a partial digital transformation." As someone who has worked in IT for many years with many global retailers, I can confidently say that if you're not going to commit 100% to the process, you might as well keep your in-person call centers and leave your business back in the 1980s.

I come from a large, blended family, so communication has always been important. I always have several large group chats going across various platforms depending on who's in them. Moving my entire family to one central chat/voice/email system has been a lifesaver. I don't have to follow threads from 10 different aunties from system to system or thread to thread. It's all in one place now.

At work, I flagged this potential problem to my employer and insisted that we focus on integrating UC with CC before we rolled out any digital solutions, so we at least had a plan. I fully support phasing any digital migration, but we can't just sit here and not have a plan to unify our internal and external communications.

Fortunately, my company moved to a cloud platform, which allowed us to implement a true omnichannel experience and incorporate our back-office employees into the process. We started by deploying voice and email applications but planned to implement more of the portfolio to support our agents, employees, and customers.

It's a huge improvement over our previous platform. Agents can access email directly from the platform, and we can easily customize features. We also gained accountability: We no longer have "I got this one" messages going out to the whole team like when everyone worked from the same queue. Plus, our emails now look more professional and match our company brand. Marketing is thrilled!

At the suggestion of one of our sales directors, we recently integrated our contact center with our virtual meeting platform so employees can have 1:1 and group meetings across the globe and see the availability of their back-office counterparts without delay. Our push into full remote work makes this essential in creating employee connections, so remote doesn't have to mean isolated. The integration is straightforward and integrates well with our workflows. Since launching these features, company morale has gone up while our turnover rate has decreased. I hope to merge these workflows into our training and quality assurance departments to unify communications across all areas, not just sales and customer service.

And now that we have plans to set up all these communication functions internally, we can easily adapt them to work with our client-facing communications. As my team looks to the future, we see further integration of customer experience across all our selling services and look forward to adding chat.

We now have the right future-proofed system so we can grow with our commerce, whether via contact center or web. Chat is a first step in supporting the web experience with live agents. Our sales director is excited that we'll soon be able to route customers at any point in their journey on the channel of their choice: voice, video, chat, messaging, email, and social. And now that we have the front office (the contact center) tied nicely into the back office, even questions that require an expert are solved quickly. We're confident adding more channels won't slow us down. Experts are standing by.

If my years in IT have taught me anything, it's not only about offering the newest technology to our customers. It's about offering the widest variety of communication options. If you're a global brand, you're trying to cast the widest net for your customer base. People all have their own communication preferences. I know I will never reach my wife on chat; she communicates purely through voice and email. But my step kids? If it isn't a chat under 40 characters, I'll never hear back. You have to meet people where they are.

eBonding

Most integrations focus on the exchanging of data — sending data between two applications via web services. Bridging, or eBonding, integrations facilitate data transmission, but they're a bit more sophisticated than the colloquial definition of integration. A term that's gaining in popularity, eBonding refers to a type of system-to-system communication. As of this writing, ServiceNow leads the way in the promotion and usage of the term, but it's beginning to adopt a more colloquial use — like how people use AI to describe anything "smart," whether or not there's actually an AI or machine learning (ML) algorithm behind it.

eBonding differs from traditional event-based system synchronization in two ways:

- First, with eBonded applications, both are considered the source of truth. This contrasts with typical integrations where one system typically asks the other "primary" data source for information. With eBonding, the data appears local to all the systems.
- Second, the timing of the integration sets it apart. The syncing of eBonded applications happens automatically instead of based on a separately triggered event. Essentially, eBonding happens whether or not a change occurs. (Other integrations happen when an event occurs.)

With eBonding the rule set is between two applications, not between one and many. So, the eBonding "protocol" helps two independent applications define and "bond," a "ticket" of a particular type. eBonding requires no middleware, per se; it's more of an edge capability that at least one of the platforms must have for it to work. One of the two applications needs to establish the handshaking protocol for this to work — ServiceNow has that. I think of this handshaking protocol as a software development toolkit (SDK[33]) of sorts. So, while it requires effort from both platforms, it doesn't require both platforms to have an explicitly defined eBonding protocol. If the second one doesn't have an eBonding protocol, the setup work will just involve mapping its APIs to the SDK provided by the other.

Contact centers offer opportunities to streamline with eBonding due to the dynamic nature of the data involved. If your team edits information directly into a system that depends heavily on the data of an application that's maintained and frequently modified by another team on another platform, eBonding might help

---

[33] Software development kits are a collection of software development tools in one installable package.

reduce complexity of the integration. While I haven't seen eBonding implemented widely inside the contact center yet, I'm excited to see how and where this technology will mature.

PROCESS PIONEERS

Joleen Encounters an Incompatible CRM Flub

After landing her dream job as the chief sales technologist of a software development startup, Joleen's first task was to build on its cloud contact center efforts and replace the existing on-premises CRM with a new cloud solution. What should have been a seamless process turned into a nightmare when incompatibility between the company's contact center platform and the new CRM halted contact center operations. To make matters worse, a troublemaking colleague used the experience to suggest Joleen didn't deserve her role.

Joleen: I was with my mom when I received the call that I had been hired. Just like that we were dancing in the kitchen. I had been dreaming of this opportunity for months: a chance to work with a promising startup where I could have meaningful impact. I loved my previous job, but it's hard to measure your contribution to the overall picture in a big corporation.

I started immediately as Chief Sales Technologist. I hadn't even heard of the role until I saw the listing with "responsible for overseeing sales strategies, directing the resources, and ensuring that our sales technology aligns with business goals." It was perfect.

During the interview, I asked about how much traffic the company was currently getting and how they were managing it. I deduced that we needed to replace CRM software as my first order of business.

To start, it was an on-prem CRM, which was challenging because the company was looking to switch to a hybrid working model. Moreover, the existing solution had limited integration capabilities, which resulted in customer and lead data being spread over multiple databases. There wasn't a simple way to combine the data into useful profiles. Its only redeeming feature was a custom integration for the up-and-coming web-based call center application.

I didn't hesitate to call for a meeting after my onboarding sessions. I soon realized things might not go as smoothly as I had imagined. One of my new coworkers made it clear that she didn't think it was a good idea. Wendy felt we should switch to the cloud version of the current CRM because it was cheaper, would take less time, and people wouldn't have to learn a new system. They were all valid points, albeit delivered condescendingly.

I went on to explain that her option might make sense in the short term, but current growth rates suggested we'd need a CRM replacement like Microsoft Dynamics sooner rather than later. The cloud version of the existing CRM would solve only a handful of integration issues. In the end, leadership agreed with me and approved the switch. I had a sense Wendy still had some mischief in mind. I didn't have to wait too long to confirm my suspicions.

Shortly after we set up the CRM and were working on integrations with other business solutions, I discovered that we couldn't integrate the contact center with the new CRM. The whole point of replacing the CRM was to empower the contact center to close more sales.

I couldn't believe I had missed such a critical detail. In retrospect, I shouldn't have assumed that a cloud-based solution would be CRM-agnostic. But given the size of the vendor they had chosen, it wasn't surprising that it lacked a diverse set of integrations. But the worst part was that Wendy knew it all along and chose to withhold the information from me.

I went into full panic mode. Anyone that has switched CRMs knows how hectic it can get. I hadn't slept enough in days and I was barely eating. And now I had a bigger decision: Go back to the CRM or change the existing contact center platform.

I chose the contact center. It wasn't part of the original plan, but the existing one wouldn't have scaled enough in the long term anyway.

Leads were coming in droves: Every minute of contact center downtime was another minute that we were losing money. It wasn't the first impression I'd hoped to make. Luckily, my bosses were quite understanding. In fact, all the pressure fell on Wendy. Because she was the one who had recommended the previous CRM and the contact center solution, she understood their limitations more than anybody.

With that in mind, I met with her and had a very mature conversation. I won't say we became besties, but there's mutual respect between us. If not for her help, it would have taken much longer to find a new contact center replacement. She knew the company more than I did, but I was more versed about available solutions.

It was all a blessing in disguise. The idea to change CRMs was good and necessary, but combining it with the new platform was the game changer. It has brought so many benefits. For instance, when an agent gets an inbound call from a customer or lead, Microsoft Dynamics automatically displays all the customer data on the agent's desktop, which helps the agent provide a personalized experience. We estimate that alone has increased revenue by 14%. What's more, unlike the previous contact center, ours will work with any CRM we choose. Not that we'll change anytime soon, but it's nice to know we can.

CHAPTER SEVEN

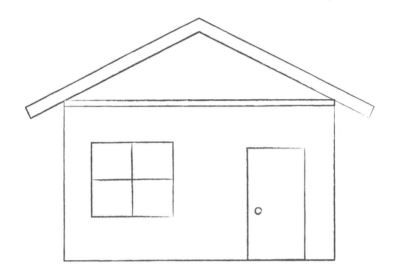

THE "BASE" BUILD

Have you ever walked into an open house or watched a home improvement show and thought to yourself: "Wow, this is all sooo builder-grade!"? I think we've all stood in a room surrounded by beige, unoffensive finishes that no one really loves, but — technically — work. Contractors know they're not impressing anyone with builder-grade finishes, but they also know most people will be "fine" with the generic finishes.

It's no different in the contact center. Base builds will cover certain "out of the box" use cases. And just like house builders, different contactors have different levels of base finishes. Some might provide "decorator ready" interiors where the kitchens and baths are installed, but the rest of the home lacks flooring and paint. Others might go further, offering a generic furniture package — providing you a place to sit while you figure out the rest.

A Dream Home with No Drywall

Work with the relevant business units to decide what's best for your business. In my experience, IT preferences vary wildly from those of individual business units. Your team might feel that "designer ready" sounds great; you can customize the whole thing to reflect the preferences of the business. However, anyone who has walked into an empty house — I'm talking exposed framing — and then been asked: "How would you like us to put it together?" knows it's a lot to take on.

If you deliver a dream home with no drywall to a room full of people expecting a "just bring your toothbrush" situation, they'll be disappointed, and the project will fail. So, survey all involved parties and determine how they imagine the "base build." That will help you determine whether you should consider a platform, prebuilt, or a hybrid solution. Since we don't know what we don't know, let's discuss the merits of each strategy.

Platform

In our analogy, a solution provider that delivers framing without drywall is a platform. Solutions like Amazon Connect and Twilio fall into this category. They provide all the tools and APIs you need to build a final solution precisely to your own requirements.

The problem is platform-only solutions often require a systems integrator like Deloitte or Kyndryl to implement successfully because your IT department won't have the bandwidth and your business units lack the expertise to code. This slows your time to value and puts the expertise in the hands of a third party. It also places a large burden on the team that must now make a lot of design decisions that they're likely underprepared to make.

Prebuilt

At the other end of the spectrum, we find the pre-furnished apartments. In the contact center, these prebuilt solutions are often designed for a specific industry or use case. The vendor will need some idea what kind of sofa you'd like, but if they have one in stock, they'll set it all up before you arrive. Vendors like Glia and Gryphon.ai are examples. They can be a great option if your business is new to running a contact center.

But what if the prebuilt configuration doesn't work or is just too uncomfortable to live with? Someone will have to remove that ugly, templatized sofa. And that someone is probably you. How much time will you waste undoing work before you can make it your own? Can you even make it your own? Many prebuilt solutions lack the flexibility and administrative tools you'd need to tailor things to your business's needs.

We caution against following the siren song of a prebuilt solution as the initial deployment speed comes at the cost of future agility.

Hybrid

In true Goldilocks fashion, hybrid solutions offer the best of both strategies. These are your "decorator-ready" apartments with the basics and maybe some pre-packaged finishing options, but they also welcome the flexibility to give you what you actually need.

In a true hybrid solution — like those offered by Five9 and NICE — you will find:

- Vast configuration options
  - Industry expertise and example use cases
  - Clicks-not-code administrative interfaces
  - APIs to extend and configure the solution
- Reporting for everyone
  - Templatized sample reports
  - Business-user-friendly data exploration
  - Custom reporting solutions
  - Integration to corporate data lakes
- A variety of user experiences to suit every department's unique needs

- Easy integration to third-party applications
  - Productized CRM integrations
  - SDKs to extend to other applications
- Simple administration, configuration, and training of AI, automation, and analytics

The key advantage of a hybrid solution is that you choose how much effort to put into it. Use templates as a jumping-off point. Use APIs to build bespoke solutions. Let one department enjoy the autonomy of business-user–friendly administration while another partners with your team to optimize for what it needs.

For IT, this allows you to turn projects over to the business unit once they're complete. That level of freedom keeps your business agile — moving at the speed of the industry.

Time to Return

Time is an overlooked component of return-on-investment (ROI) calculations. After 10 years in sales, the only time I heard anyone mention "time to ROI" was on the *Shark Tank* reruns I watched in my hotel room. The time it takes for an implementation to return value to the business should absolutely be part of the decision calculus.

Consider the time it takes to initially go live. Will this phase offer a return, or is it just a "keep the lights on" phase? Then consider the time until completion of the final phase of the rollout. What value milestones will you pass along the way? And what application components do you need to pay for during the limbo of implementation?

As an aside, Salesforce.com, for example, is famous for forcing customers to pay for 100% of the contracted user counts from day 1, with no regard or sympathy for the fact that it often takes months for a business to deploy their solution. That's potentially thousands of dollars of lost value while you wait for an implementation to conclude. Not all vendors' contracts are so black and white; some allow you to pay as you realize, or ramp toward, value.

Now, returning to the topic of time to value, remember: Patience is a virtue. I'm not suggesting that the fastest vendor is the best one. I'm suggesting you get what you pay for and there's a balance between rapid deployment and thoughtful reimagination.

If your existing platform is hard down, dead, and no amount of turning it off and on again will help, you need that new platform to stand up over the weekend. It needs to deliver immediate value. As in RIGHT NOW. But we both know that the initial implementation won't be the final one. Once you've put out the fire and the communication lines open again, you can take a second look at how else the platform will provide value to your org. Measure that.

PROCESS PIONEERS

Franny Gets Fried by an RFP

Franny is the contact center operations manager at a tax preparation and fintech company. As the company's contract with its contact center provider was about to end, Franny looked to switch providers. She was keen on getting the perfect solution and believed that a request for proposal (RFP) would help her achieve that. Unfortunately, in her attempt to get the solution with the best features, she ended up with one that didn't align with her company's goals.

Franny: When I look back, my decision to issue an RFP wasn't a bad one. It's how I went about it. Last time, we settled for a vendor without fully understanding the offer. We wound up with thousands of dollars of hidden costs in the two years we worked together. The plan we chose hadn't included long-distance charges. As an online finance company, we serve clients from all states, and we recently we expanded to Canada and Australia.

Now that the contract was expiring, I was committed to not repeat the mistake. I emphasized a breakdown of the pricing model in the RFP along with a list of required features such as support for multiple integrations, reporting capabilities, AI-supported functionalities, and compliance adherence. And therein came the problem.

All these features are critical and can provide competitive advantage. But do you know what's more important? Ensuring that the platform functionalities truly align with your company's operational and marketing goals. My mistake was outlining a list of features without considering how they addressed problems at the contact center.

I failed to properly outline my short- and long-term business goals in the RFP. As a result, I got mostly generic proposals that didn't mention how they would align to our business model. At the time, I didn't see a problem as long they had all the right features.

And that's how I ended up choosing a solution that was incompatible with our company. I was so confident that I got our chief marketing officer to approve it without question. Then we started planning the implementation. And the holes started appearing.

Most glaring was that although the platform had all the features I wanted, several required third-party integrations. And using the AI-powered features and workflow management required us to work outside the main interface. Research has shown that switching between programs during work significantly reduces agent productivity. The groans of my team during the training demos only confirmed that finding.

I had made another bad decision: hours writing the RFP, weeks going through product demos and proofs of concept from shortlisted vendors, and days of planning migration — wasted.

Now I had to decide:

- Proceed with implementing this new platform and look for a way to make it work?
- Go back to the drawing board and find a solution that better fits our business?

What if I chose the latter and wound up with another incompatible solution? That's more time and resources wasted.

Just when I thought there was no winning for me, I got a call that changed everything. The timing was just perfect. A sales rep from one of the short-listed vendors called to follow up on the project.

At that point, I was nearing a breaking point. I explained my predicament: I had chosen a platform based on the promise of bells and whistles at an amazing price. But things were not going as expected.

The rep wasn't surprised. They said that, after seeing my RFP, they'd felt I was going about the process the wrong way but felt they couldn't address the issue without violating the rules of the RFP. So, they just responded as best they could, hoping I'd realize there's more to vendor-customer relationships than what shows up on paper.

The rep said that my approach was like that of a man trying to use a checklist to evaluate a future wife. One woman may meet all his standards — well-educated, beautiful hair, nice smile, loves sports, etc. — but that doesn't mean that the relationship will work. It doesn't mean she'll find him to be a perfect match. Had I not been under so much stress, it would have made me laugh.

The conversation made me realize another critical error. I hadn't involved other departments in the selection process.

Our legal and HR teams constantly interact with the contact center. I went on to explain in detail what I was hoping to achieve. The vendor had a plan to help us achieve the spirit of the project, not just deliver a literal list of features.

Fortunately, we hadn't started migrating data to the other vendor's solution. I decided to switch vendors. And by focusing on the big picture rather than just the features, we ended up with a better solution that has completely transformed not just our contact center, but our entire company. It's a lesson I had to learn the hard way.

Who's Doing the Work?

Just because you can paint your own house, doesn't mean you have (or want) to. Everyone has their own level of comfort when it comes to DIYing. Sometimes it's just easier to do it than to explain the specifics of an entire project to someone who is unfamiliar with your style or preferences. And other times, the peace of mind that comes from knowing an expert will complete the job is more than worth the time you spend sharing the vision.

Small businesses, those with limited IT resources, and companies running very lean may not have time to do the work themselves. On the other hand, a BPO[34] will likely invest the time to learn all the nuance of their selected contact center platform, to become the ultimate DIYer. With clients coming and going all the time, it makes perfect sense to cut out the middle tier and directly build what their clients need. In fact, as a BPO, the inability to rapidly deploy client-specific configurations can seriously hinder business.

Large enterprises with many business units should follow the lead of our BPO friends. Each business unit needs to adapt to the changes demanded by its clients. Investing the time and resources

---

[34] A business process outsourcer offers the staffing part of contact center services, often to multiple clients or businesses.

is warranted by the benefits yielded by the agility it affords. But that doesn't mean you have to do it all yourself right out of the gate.

What to Expect from Your Contractor (Vendor)

When first switching to a new solution, you don't know what you don't know. We might think we have a good idea of the solution we want, but our past experiences will always shape our opinions. It's the same with the vendor's opinions: Their professional services team has seen it all. I'm reminded of the Farmers Insurance commercials with J. K. Simmons where he says, "We know a thing or two, because we've seen a thing or two."

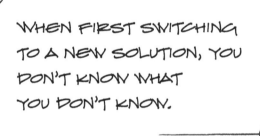

WHEN FIRST SWITCHING TO A NEW SOLUTION, YOU DON'T KNOW WHAT YOU DON'T KNOW.

Among other things, you can expect your vendor's implementation team to:

- Know the features better than you (at least initially)
- Combine their previous client experiences with your requirements to offer better solutions
- Provide fresh perspective on your challenges

Let's say your business is all about socks. Your company sells, manufactures, and distributes socks. You are a sock expert. Even your IT and human resources teams know more than their fair share about socks and sock enthusiasts. It's the business.

Contact center is its own business. It's an industry. Don't expect your team, even the team of sock supporters to also be contact center experts. Your vendor should provide relevant guidance, best practices, support, and expertise for the contact center so your team can do what it does best: knocking our socks off.

Can We DIY?

Yes! Always expect capabilities that support your independence. In fact, expect capabilities that support the leaders of individual business units to handle their own adds, moves, and changes.

At the very least, your selected solution should empower you to independently:

- Update call flows and intelligent virtual agents
- Add/remove users
- Create and run reports (even custom ones)
- Modify screen pops and other employee enablement elements
- Configure and train AI capabilities
- Access training and support

Everything the vendor's professional services team does (mechanically) you should be able to do yourself. Use the services team for their expertise and the time savings that come with managed services, not because it's the only option.

Systems Integrators (SIs)

Systems integrators — consultants from firms like Accenture, Deloitte, Kyndryl, and Slalom — offer consulting and implementation services for large-scale, business transformation projects and can provide your organization rich perspective. Much like we've (hopefully) inspired your IT organization to take a holistic approach that counsels and consults your line-of-business leaders, SIs bring a holistic approach, at a larger scale, with more industry experience. Unfortunately, SIs typically don't have deep contact center operations knowledge, so be sure you include your trusted vendor advisors in the conversation. Additionally, the guidance in this book will help ensure you don't miss any technical details.

SIs add a lot of value in their holistic approach to business transformation. If you're already working with an SI in another aspect of your organization, it can help to loop them into the contact center transformation. Their methodical, yet big-picture approach can result in better alignment across your various teams and deliver better customer experience.

If you don't have an SI but think one would be beneficial, your CCaaS vendor likely has relationships with the larger firms. They can help introduce you to a partner that understands both your industry and contact center to help guide you along your contact center transformation journey.

Is There a Warranty?

There was a trend in the 1990s and early 2000s when new home builders offered home warranties to persuade potential buyers. The idea is nice: If anything went wrong during the warranty period, the builder would correct it. But these types of programs often went bankrupt, leaving the homeowners footing the bill.

It wasn't entirely the result of faulty craftmanship. For instance, a brand-new home built on a solid concrete slab will start to settle into the soil around it. That settling will cause some cracks in the plaster around your door or window frames. It's not the builder's fault, it's gravity. And you can't fight gravity!

The problem with builders using warranties to earn instant trust with a buyer is in the word instant. Trust is earned over time. Greet anyone who's trying to rush you to trust them with lofty promises or empty warranties — which, in the software world, manifest as lofty, unrealistic SLA offers — with a hefty dose of skepticism. A vendor that has earned the trust of its customers will have documented testimonials, case studies, and published historical uptime statistics, not just a smile-and-a-wink SLA.

Service Level Agreements (SLAs)

In the uptime section of Chapter 2, we discussed the calculation of uptime and established that "five nines" of availability — 99.999%

uptime — is considered the gold standard for telephony solutions. I understand the impulse to seek a company that offers an SLA in excess of that. But it's not the number of nines that makes an SLA valuable. The teeth of the agreement comes from penalties the vendor pays when it doesn't meet the SLA. An empty promise of 100% uptime — aside from being unrealistic — means nothing if all you get is a (quasi) sincere apology for the inconvenience of downtime.

SLAs are great negotiation levers for both you and the vendor. If the occasional five-minute-long outage won't cost your business too much (customers or hard dollars), then consider negotiating elsewhere in your deal. It might not make sense to demand huge penalties or an "extra" nine.

As you approach this topic, first try to assess how likely it is that the vendor will deliver on the uptime it's promising. Does it publish historical uptime statistics? Is it transparent about its audiences? And most important, how does the vendor calculate uptime? You might be surprised to discover that some companies don't use a typical *(minutes of system availability)* ÷ *(minutes in the day)* calculation.

Every system will experience downtime. The more important statistic is the mean time to resolution. The support team's SLAs are a decent indicator. But to really evaluate your expected mean time to resolution, you'll need to understand how well the vendor's support performs when you experience an outage or other business-impacting issue.

Support

Support comes in many flavors. Every CCaaS solution should include a base level of 24x7 support in the subscription license. So, the first step to evaluating a vendor's support is to understand what you get "out of the box." This will vary by vendor.

Don't be quick to assume that it's bad when one vendor charges extra for something that another includes for free. Evaluate the total cost of ownership based on what you need. I guarantee that cost, while perhaps not a line item, is reflected somewhere in the overall solution price. Resist the urge to compare support as a line item. Instead focus on what your business needs to accomplish and the kind of support you need to get there.

"Premium" Support

Let's assume the base support package includes "basic" break-fix support. Vendors all brand their premium support offerings under different names, so don't get hung up on the word premium. For the purposes of this conversation, premium support refers to a level of service that goes beyond basic 24x7 break-fix support and will fall into two categories: pooled and dedicated.

- Pooled premium support connects you with a group of agents who are assigned to your account. You may have specific point of contact, but you're generally supported by an around-the-clock team that also supports other customers. The team gets to know your business, which allows you to develop a shorthand for communication and get to the heart of your issues more quickly. These specialized agents also typically go beyond break-fix. Depending on the contract, you may be eligible for administration support, monthly or quarterly business reviews, help with reporting, and more.

- Dedicated premium support offers all the benefits of the above, minus the sharing. If your organization's size warrants full-time dedicated support resources, CCaaS vendors are generally happy to oblige.

Technical Account Management Services

Technical account managers (TAMs) are another flavor of shared-yet-dedicated resources. These are solution experts who support a very limited number of clients. They bring industry and product expertise to help guarantee you get the most from your solution investment. If your IT department intends to be hands-off following the purchase decision, a TAM is a must-have. TAMs offer the sounding-board guidance, hands-on support, release reviews (to ensure the team capitalizes on new features), and single-point-of-contact that line-of-business owners need to maximize their contact center investments.

Third-Party or Partner-Delivered Support

If you purchase a CCaaS solution through a reseller, there's a good chance that partner will deliver the level 1 and 2 support. This can be a good thing. Your team might already have a relationship with the partner's support organization, making it natural to turn to them for help with other business applications. Things to watch:

- Verify that the reseller is a certified support partner of your CCaaS vendor.
- Make sure there's a clear escalation path for support issues extending beyond their direct control.
- Understand the related SLAs for various types of support cases.

Education and Training

It'd be silly to sell someone a solution and not train them on it. If your vendor doesn't offer at least some training as part of your implementation, it's time to run! (And don't look back.)

Don't forget about day 2 or day 100 training. Contact centers experience incredibly high turnover rates. Although a good solution will include capabilities to help mitigate attrition, you'll still likely train new hires on a weekly or monthly basis.

Online training portals, self-paced lessons, live webinars, and fee-based onsite training should all be options to educate your teams.

David Meets the Devil in the Details

An IT director of a multinational fast-food organization, David inherited a contact center nightmare. Unfortunately, the replacement project's urgency and a soft spot for a good burger left him back where he started.

David: It's better to rip off a bandage than slowly tear it away, right? I'm in charge of the back-end and communication networks for a fast-casual restaurant chain. Instead of preparing the food, greeting customers, and mopping the floor, I support the system handling phone calls and online orders. It's all about efficiency. And in the burger business, that's even more pronounced.

We strive to always be more efficient by discovering ways to shave off seconds in production, analyzing data to see trends, updating our tools in a smooth manner, and so on. When things work better, it just feels better.

Our call-routing infrastructure was old enough to start college — and we all know how pricey college can get. It sort of worked, but now and then, incidents resulted in long wait times on the phone or a customer would bail out.

And our system didn't gather meaningful data. We couldn't trace self-service calls to locations or see details such as at which point the customer hung up or the amount of time the customer spent waiting. It's important data that could optimize our performance.

So, it was time for this system to matriculate on out of here. We needed something more up-to-date. Naturally, I sought a cost-efficient-yet-robust solution, but speedy implementation was the biggest priority.

I spent months buried in offers from different providers, all suggesting tons of features and add-ons. It was hard to track it all. Ultimately, a local upstart emerged as the victor. It had a base package with a short implementation time and options to add features in the future.

My sales rep James was chatty and energetic, like a Border Collie. He also had this superpower to eat a burger without making a mess while discussing his business proposal. He knew all the best burger spots. It was an efficient meeting, to say the least. As I pointed out the nationwide scale of the project and my desire for things to be done quickly, he said it wouldn't be a problem. He didn't provide specific references but assured me they had done this before.

The initial results were great. James encouraged us to go with a phased implementation, which seemed to pay off. His team worked so fast. We completed the initial wave of the implementation ahead of schedule. We met every week at a different burger shop, and I thought everything was going splendidly. My wife, on the other hand, wondered why a person who works with phones and video chats insisted on in-person meetings. I didn't think much of it then, but now I see James's aversion to email might've been a warning sign.

As we approached phase 2, it got more difficult to get time with James. My team started to ask about when they would receive the advanced features they needed. While the base system routing calls was impressive and installed really quickly, getting access to the additional features turned out to be an ordeal. Suddenly the vendor needed to install hardware on-site in each individual store across the country — and bill all the travel and expenses back to me.

I was stunned reading the explanation on why this was necessary. And I physically flinched when I came to the part about how long it would take and how much it would cost. I sent back a rebuttal, wanting to meet in person. Now, James insisted we should keep our exchanges through email. Interestingly, his typed words weren't as confident as those with a burger in his hand.

I realized that he and his company had simply promised more than it could handle. The solution sounded great, but the features didn't back up the stories. He was all marketing and no follow-through.

In the end, we chose to rip off the bandage (again) and start over. Our current, much more experienced vendor really made it work — and the additional ideas they lent us regarding IVA use are paying off. I still feel silly for being blinded by burgers. But at least I get to share my story and we can all learn from the experience. Now I know — always get a reference and make sure you know what's really included in each phase of the rollout.

CHAPTER EIGHT

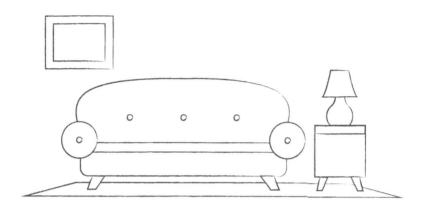

SELECTING A FURNITURE PACKAGE

Good news! By now you have a really good idea of what type of contact center solution will work well for your organization. You understand how to represent your constituencies, earn their trust, and when to get your business units involved (early and often!). Now it's time to invite in a decorator.

Before you can move your teams into this contact center forever home, you need "furniture." In our metaphor, furniture, like in life, will come in many forms:

- First, we'll want to think about the entryway and living rooms: the customer experience.
- Then we'll consider everything from kitchen tables to bedroom sets to make sure the contact center staff has everything it needs.
- Finally, we'll explore the options to make your contact center a "smart home" and how adding AI, automation, and analytics will improve everyone's experience.

Define the Customer Experience

One of the biggest mistakes people make when moving to a new platform is continuing to design using an inside-out approach. When they first came out, the primary use case of IVRs was to help distribute and deflect calls. They were implemented using the inside-out approach of: "How can we reduce the number of calls that make it to an agent?"

This is a great idea from an efficiency standpoint, but it led to an era of terrible customer experiences and an entire generation of people who dread calling customer support.

You might be thinking: "But efficiency is a primary motivator for our making a change!" You're not alone. Many, if not most, companies mature their contact center deployments by tackling operational efficiency before moving on to improving the efficacy of their teams, and — finally — focusing on creating more engaging customer experiences. Efficiency, efficacy, engagement: It's a great journey, one I hope you take. But how efficient can your phone system be if the customers refuse to use it as designed?

Adopt an Outside-In Approach

Take the time to consider the customers' perspective. If you briefly view things from the outside in and spend a moment in their shoes, you'll save considerable time and headache later.

Consider a situation where you want to provide 10 customer self-service options because those 10 use cases create the most busywork for your staff. You'd be much more efficient if you could automate them, right? This sounds like a great plan! Ten opportunities to automate?!? Sign me up.

Adopting the outside-in approach requires only that you stop and consider the customers' experience when you present them with 10 options. Will you make them listen to a list of all 10 before they can select one? Will you design an experience that only saves you time by wasting someone else's? What kind of experience would you prefer? Then design from there.

The result might be a system that uses CRM data to pare the list down to items the specific caller is likely to need. Imagine an electrical company that recognizes Ralph's number, analyzes the last few times he's called, and leads with "Hi Ralph, calling about another down power line?" Versus when Vivian rings up, "Hello Vivian, may I help you set up autopay?" (Because it knew she had searched for that on the company website earlier that day.) I long for a system that doesn't present me with options that don't apply or offers that it should know I'm ineligible for. "Yes, I am aware that I can pay online, I do it every month!"

Another option is an application that uses natural language or word-spotting technologies to allow the caller to tell you why they're calling before you rattle off a long list of options. Basically, a phone system that greets a customer with "Hi, Erin. What's up?" and only makes us suffer through a menu of options when I ask for something obscure.

This is an area where IT can really lend a fresh perspective. Imagine you're a customer of your company. Put aside how you know it works today and ask:

- How would I like to reach out for help?
- What type of experience would I expect?
- What would make me smile? Or frown?

Then discuss with the business how the choices they make during design will impact the satisfaction goals by which they're likely measured. Customer satisfaction starts before an agent ever gets on the line.

Customer Experience (CX) That Wows

Customers are just people. People that you need to keep your business afloat? Sure. People you need to impress? Yes. People who are a lot less forgiving these days? Absolutely. But still, they are people.

Customers have simple, predictable needs and desires. If you respect their time, intelligence, and history, they will respect and reward your efforts.

Respect Their Time

Solutions like IVAs help you balance internal desires to automate with respecting the customer's time. IVAs don't get sick, tired, or take time off. They serve your customers 24x7. They're available essentially whenever the customer wants on any channel — voice, chat, messenger, SMS, etc. — and can be quite conversational.

Respect Their Intelligence

Most customers attempt to solve problems on their own before reaching out to your company. They will use your online trouble-shooter, check blogs or Reddit, and ask Dr. Google before reaching out to obtain help directly.

Your team can witness some of this effort and code to address it. For example, if someone initiates a chat from an FAQ page or an online tutorial, don't immediately suggest they check out the FAQ. Respect them enough to assume they've already tried that step. Or, at the very least, phrase the response like: "I'm sorry <this article> didn't help, let's try <this> instead." That way you can casually provide the obvious answer while still respecting their search efforts. Either way, select a solution that can use web analytics or customer journey data to adjust the experience you serve them.

Respect Their History

You should know your customers. You have the data. You can personalize service with simple things like greeting people by name, having their latest order number ready, or anticipating a problem because others using the same product or in the same service area are experiencing issues. As with journey analytics, the importance of integration surfaces. Your new cloud platform should accommodate all the next-generation expectations your customers have.

We're all influenced by algorithms that streaming services and online retailers use to anticipate our next desire for programming and product. A thought-leading contact center solution will have tools (at least in the works) that help you meet these expectations. Know your customer better and show them you care with rich integrations and machine-learning capabilities scaled for and delivered to everyone.

Hot CX Journeys for Industry Verticals

With customer expectations and technology changing so quickly, your business partners may struggle to imagine how to get the most from contact center technology.

The following are examples of customer journeys that leading companies in healthcare, retail, and government use to define the dream as they strive to make it a reality. I hope you will find inspiration and a partner to help you bring them to life.

Also consider how deploying IVAs can help you add support for more languages, thereby reaching more patients, customers, or constituents through your contact center.

Healthcare (Providers)

As patients increasingly approach the healthcare journey like they approach other decisions — researching options online in advance of acting — providers are borrowing lessons from retail. In fact, at the most recent customer experience conference I attended, a representative from a large health insurance provider joined a discussion session aimed at retail companies because they wanted to learn the lessons their retail peers had to offer.

Healthcare providers seeking to reintroduce themselves into the "shopping for care" journey have considered using AI and automation to:

- Self-diagnose with a bot
- Provide after-hours, multichannel support
- Match doctors and patients by closest facility, appointment availability, or facility type (telehealth, clinic, or urgent care)
- Help patients verify benefits or insurance acceptance
- Provide cost estimates (especially relevant in the United States given the No Surprises Act)
- Accept requests for callback after hours
- Send documents for completion, such as patient history, HIPAA acknowledgement, consent forms, etc.

Once a patient joins a provider, AI and automation can continue to help streamline the patient experience. Healthcare orgs are utilizing the contact center to increase efficiency in a variety of ways, including:

Patient Access

- Perform screening and triage conversations
- Streamline the intake process through validating insurance, accepting co-pays, and processing documents for signature
- Schedule treatment
- Schedule transportation
- Send appointment reminders
- Do rescheduling, if needed

Treatment

- Send pre-visit reminders like: Don't drink water after midnight

- Answer FAQs such as:
  - Where to park or which building to enter
  - When to arrive — personalized, based on patient's scheduled procedure
  - What can family members expect / where can they wait
  - Patient pickup procedures
- Provide post-discharge documents
- Handle pharmacy orders
- Take payment

Recovery

The hospital of the future is at home; people recover better at home. So, healthcare leaders are looking for ways to enable in-home recovery. Consider using contact center technology to:

- Manage chronic care and medical devices with integrations and alerts
- Leverage health-tracking apps as a contact center point of presence
- Provide proactive follow-up and communication, including scheduling appointments and sending reminders
- Answer FAQs such as:
  - Where to get rehab center information
  - When to ask for help
  - What's next
- Offer rural-area remote support and patient monitoring
- Perform post-discharge follow-up check-ins
  - How are they feeling?
  - Have they taken medication?
- Schedule prescription refills

Revenue Cycle: Payment Collection
- Send payment reminders
- Offer secure payment via IVA
- Connect with a financial counselor

One of the more exciting use cases is the use of speech patterns to identify health issues. Is the caller having trouble breathing? Speaking? Is there hoarseness compared to a baseline voiceprint? I don't know of an organization that's there yet, but current AI advancements make use cases like these much more plausible than they were several years ago. Neat stuff.

Retail

Think about the last time you bought something. Did you begin by calling a salesperson? Unlikely. You probably searched online. And that's a problem for retailers. With all the research already done by the time a prospect reaches out, the sales motion is different.

Think about buying a car today. Do you rely on the dealership salesperson to tell you about the car? Or will you do most of the research online and select your new vehicle in advance? Salespeople no longer facilitate information gathering; they mostly handle contracts and objection handling — and maybe the occasional test drive.

Retailers large and small have realized the importance of social communities where people can discuss their needs with their peers or neighbors. Whether looking for a dentist or bagels, people want to know the outcome going in. So, how can you use that in the contact center?

Should retailers cruise for information on social media to — as the slogan goes — join the conversation? Or should a business participate in conversations only when a customer speaks directly to them, not just about them? Some enterprises are avoiding this ethical ambiguity by trying to manage the conversation platform. By encouraging the creation of micro-communities and hosting the dialogues, they hope to bring the customer conversation back where they can influence it.

Whichever side of the fence your company sits on, your contact center agents need information from these conversations. IT can help by designing the information flow to ensure agents have all the conversational context, even elements that weren't with the contact center directly.

Another way the contact center can transform the retail experience is by embracing the brand's ambassador. Today, if I think memorable brand ambassadors, I think of the GEICO gecko, Jan the peppy lady from the Toyota ads, Flo from Progressive Insurance, and Lily from the AT&T commercials. But if I call their contact center, am I greeted by a virtual agent with their voice and personality? (Not the last time I checked.)

But why not? Technology exists today where you can use a real person's voice to generate human-realistic voice prompts. It's very possible to create continuity of brand from your television commercial through web bots and the contact center. Personally, I think it'd be fun if the GEICO gecko called to remind me about my upcoming insurance renewal. I'm a sucker for his accent.

State and Local Governments

State and local governments have traditionally been slow to adopt new, cloud-based technologies. Of course, it's clearly the result of bureaucratic red tape, not IT. ;) Nevertheless, there are a few areas where we can refresh the citizen experience from inside the contact center. Consider how you can:

- Use language and real-time translation features to help people communicate in their native language so you can serve more of the community.
- Offer work-from-home options as employee groups fight to keep remote work.
- Capitalize on how the pandemic influenced people's willingness to participate in virtual meetings with union representatives, senators, and city council members.
- Offer cloud-based IT services.

Create an Empowering Employee Experience

If the goal is to make your contact center more efficient, effective, and engaging, then we're doing it backward. But as I mentioned, that's a good thing. Design with the end in mind, as they say. Having just discussed engaging customer experiences, let's now focus on how to empower your team to effectively deliver those experiences.

To discover what agents need to do their job well, you need to ask them. Yup. Ask the agents, not just their supervisors, line-of-business leaders, or project owners. Ask the people who talk directly to your customers. They know where the systems, processes, and procedures hinder instead of help. They know what customers expect and when they get impatient. They know about the data they wish they had.

During the interview process, plan to educate agents on the latest available features. Your agents don't spend their days reading blogs and industry reports to identify what features they might be missing. They are CX experts, with a possible touch of Stockholm syndrome[35]: They're used to what they know and have learned to live with it.

Ask questions that start with "what if." When an interaction arrived, what if the system delivered:

- A summary of the customer's history?
- Every option the customer had selected in the phone system?
- A warning that a customer was upset?
- Note-taking functionality?
- A nudge if you start speaking too quickly?

---

[35] Stockholm syndrome refers to a coping mechanism to a captive or abusive situation where people develop positive feelings toward their captors or abusers over time.

Then ask what features or functionality they'd want if anything was possible:

- What frustrates them most about their job?
- What makes them want to quit?
- What element of their job, if they found out software could do it for them, would cause them to break out the Champagne?
- What performance review feedback do they wish they'd received in real time instead of days or weeks later?

Maintaining Quality

An insurance provider I worked with used its quality management team to manage compliance. The whole team sweats over compliance. Auditors come in to make sure the agents complete all the necessary steps and can ding the insurance carrier rating as a result. Talk about being beholden to a checklist! So, the provider hired a whole team specifically to perform quality checks to make sure agents are on task. For them, the issue is identifying unchecked boxes. Their solution gives them two shots at compliance. First, they implemented automation that flags non-checks at the end of each interaction. Then, they use post-call analytics to double-check. For them, the stakes are so high that it's worth the extra effort to ensure quality performance and compliance.

All the efficiency and improved efficacy in the world won't matter if you lose sight of quality along the way. Your contact center's business leaders know this. They might even utilize quality management applications or programs to measure and manage their team.

- Common requests in this arena include:
- Call and/or screen recording
- Custom scorecards
- Random call sampling
- Mechanisms to share scores with agents

But those requests reflect a naïve world view of quality management. With advances in machine learning and AI, manual quality management is a waste of time. By its very nature, random sampling will produce a collection of average calls. (Because, you know, bell curves.) You don't need to listen to the average interaction, you need to find the outliers, whether terrible or excellent. Because it's in the outliers that we find teachable moments.

To find outlier interactions via a manual process, you'd end up listening to most of the interactions. Who has time for that? Instead of doubling your contact center staff to evaluate the work, apply technology for "automatic quality management" and "interaction analytics." These types of tools "listen" to 100% of your interactions. They score and analyze everything, then surface just the conversations that warrant human attention. Now your business partners can listen and coach to the trainable moments and your agents can have their whole performance evaluated.

The benefit of interaction analytics extends beyond the contact center. As a trusted advisor and strategic thinker for the company, IT should consider such a tool because it can uncover insights in many aspects of the business that departments outside the contact center need — they just don't know it. By encouraging the use of analytics, IT bridges the insights gap.

Shine a Light on Dark Data

Most quality management initiatives put the responsibility of knowing what to ask on the quality manager. The manager must search for, flag, or otherwise earmark the keywords and phrases the system should find and recognize. While the data will be helpful, it's incomplete. It's incomplete because it relies on a human to anticipate the contents of thousands of customer conversations. No one is that clairvoyant, not even Miss Cleo. To uncover the insights you don't already suspect lurk in the shadows of your contact center data, you need to use technology.

Interaction analytics, as the name suggests, can analyze every interaction that lands on the platform. Emails, chats, phone calls... you name it.

- Are customers discussing an out-of-the-ordinary topic or trend? Let the application surface that information.
- Does marketing ever ask IT to purchase a new survey tool because they want to know how customers feel about a product? Your customers have already shared their feelings in the contact center.
- Does development wonder how your products stack up to the competition and ask for big budgets for market research? We should see what your customers already say about your competitors.
- Does the sales team want to understand why some people cancel while others, in the same demographic, buy more? It's all in the interactions; you just need to shine a light on the information.

These are the kinds of cross-functional, big picture, detailed insights you can uncover with a quality interaction analytics tool. The contact center will benefit from the more efficient use of time and resources that will result in more effective individual contributors. Meanwhile, the rest of the organization will have its mind blown by the wealth of information the application brings to their attention.

Become More Efficient

Efficiency. We have finally arrived where most people start, which is to consider how a new platform will make their team(s) more efficient. To be fair, we already started this discussion when we learned about interaction analytics and automatic quality management. But that's not what most contact center platform shoppers think about when they imagine efficiency. They want their agents to perform their work faster.

The people at the heart of your contact center represent the largest part of your contact center budget. So, it's no wonder that small efficiency gains can add up to large cost savings, quickly. Review the notes from your agent interviews. I bet you'll find that a lot of things they do beg for automation. For a more methodical approach, consider the three phases of a customer interaction:

- Before the agent comes on the line — the virtual agent phase
- During the live agent interaction
- Post-call work

The Virtual Agent

IVAs are a great way to add efficiency. Adding a virtual workforce can yield a return so large that it can fund your whole digital transformation project. The math is incredible. I recently interviewed someone from Forrester Research who estimated a three-year ROI from IVA at nearly $16 million[36]. That's incredible. If you haven't already, I suggest you collaborate with your vendor to calculate the potential cost savings.

Virtual agents save agent effort by performing the mundane, repetitive, and otherwise unnecessarily time-consuming tasks. In IT, how much time does your team waste resetting passwords or turning on and off employee access to systems? What would you pay to automate that process without sacrificing security, authentication, and accountability? The contact center probably has a dozen use cases of equally low-hanging fruit, ripe for the picking.

IVAs are a must-add if you're seeking efficiency gains with a new solution. And, like I said, the gains pay for themselves.

---

[36] "The Total Economic Impact™ Of Five9," Forrester Research, July 2022
https://www.five9.com/sites/default/files/2022-10/Study_Forrester_TEI.pdf

Efficient Live Interactions

I remember one of the first times I shadowed a contact center agent, early in my sales engineering career. I arrogantly approached the exercise thinking it was silly. I'd been in the contact center space for a while and felt like I knew enough about what agents did on a daily basis. Boy was I wrong.

The reality was so much worse than I expected.

The woman I shadowed sat with a binder in her lap turned to a page detailing the latest sales promotion. Job aides littered her desk. There wasn't even room for her coffee and, judging by the coffee rings on many of the print outs, this cluttered arrangement was the norm. Her cubicle walls looked like someone trying to solve a crime on network television. As call after call arrived, I watched her eyes dart from Post-it® to paper to screen.

The whole thing was impressive, actually. She multi-tasked like a champion. But the fact that she had to made me sad. Never mind the fact that the business had to spend time and resources recruiting people with extraordinary multi-tasking skills in addition to the requisite customer service competence. What a colossal waste of time! Technology could make her job so much easier.

During your interviews of, and while shadowing, contact center staff, I'm sure you noticed several opportunities for improvement. Information that should be presented automatically. A binder easily replaced by a contextual screen pop. A paper script digitized on-screen. A Post-it swapped for real-time agent assist technology.

Your business partners are often too close to their own processes to see how terrible they are. If you don't have time — or the desire — to personally shadow agents or offer this kind of advice, ask your vendor to come on-site or do an over-the-shoulder Zoom call. As experts of their own solution, your vendors will see inefficiencies and areas for improvement. They might even do some math and help you estimate the solution ROI.

Streamline After-Call Work

After-call work is tedious but necessary. Without it, customer history won't get updated, orders might not initiate properly, and follow-up promises won't be met. But all the necessary steps — taking notes, opening tickets, saving reminders — consumes time that agents could spend serving other customers.

This is another area your contact center leaders might not realize they can streamline. Help them explore automation by discussing how other departments have tackled business process workflow automation. Encourage them to look for a CCaaS provider with a demonstrated record of streamlining after-call woes.

Common areas ripe for automation include:

- Creating call notes and summarization
- Initiating downstream workflows
  - Creating work orders
  - Scheduling future touchpoints
  - Initiating insurance claims
  - Anything that touches another team or department
- Providing/escalating product feedback
- Sending confirmation texts/emails
- Sending surveys
- Signing up customers for marketing campaigns

Many areas affect other departments or systems, which may deter some line-of-business leaders from pursuing solutions because they aren't confident in a solution's plausibility, or they don't have the political capital to spend on such collaboration. In IT, however, you do. The visibility of IT carries the perspective necessary to imagine a more streamlined future.

Look for CCaaS solutions with the capacity to integrate with several systems simultaneously and selectively — that is, trigger events conditionally. Also remember that sister systems like CRM often have their own process automation capabilities. In those cases, it might be as simple as having the contact center platform initiate an API call that triggers an already built, tested, and ready-to-go workflow.

In my experience, the best solutions employ a mix of the two: contact-center–managed workflow automation and contact-center–initiated third-party workflow automation.

Building a Smart Home

With the possible exception of my father — who refuses to allow "listening devices" in the house — everyone in my immediate orbit loves their smart speakers. I'm accustomed to asking my all-knowing Google Home for news and weather. I barely remember where I got my morning briefing before Google moved in. And, like it or not, the convenience of these devices has influenced customer and employee expectations.

When's the last time you listened to a voicemail? No need, right? Not since the transcription services got accurate. So, why are we still taking notes manually? Shouldn't all calls be automatically transcribed? (And summarized?)

Absolutely. But as with voicemail, until recently, transcription happened after the call because the time it took to process the voice stream exceeded the duration of the call. (And it was quite expensive). No longer! Real-time transcription is now commonplace. Live captioning has started appearing in collaboration tools like Zoom and Microsoft Teams.

If you look hard enough, you'll find real-time transcription in contact center solutions. And it's worth looking. Real-time transcription is the key to unlocking the dark data insights in your live, voice (audio) interactions. It's the driving force behind meaningful application of AI-powered solutions in the contact center.

Artificial Intelligence

In some ways, AI is just now starting to live up to the promises made in the first 20 years of this century. As of this writing, the solutions coming from companies like Open.ai challenge the Turing test for the first time. The idea that a computer can generate responses that exhibit intelligent behavior equivalent to, or indistinguishable from, that of a human — that I can be tricked by a generative AI algorithm — really excites me.

Set aside any personal disappointments you may have previously experienced while attempting to implement AI. We've reached a period where the computers are fast enough, memory is cheap enough, and the data is plentiful enough for AI to really deliver.

So, where does AI belong in the contact center? Where can it add value? Just about everywhere.

The most visible use case — and by that, I mean one of the "showiest" areas of demonstration — is during live-call interactions. Imagine an agent receiving real-time coaching that instructs them to slow their rate of speech, change their tone, or try an alternative sales tactic. Not from their manager, from the AI. These solutions are available today.

Next up, I expect to see real-time translation of voice — something I've been waiting for since I first watched Jim Henson's sci-fi television series *Farscape* as a kid. In it, characters had a "translator microbe," a bug-like creature, implanted into their brain that could translate anything they heard, in any language, into their native tongue. Instantly. In the case of the main character, it was as if everyone spoke English. Flawless, real-time translation. Wow.

(If you missed *Farscape*, you might remember the Babel fish from *The Hitchhiker's Guide to the Galaxy* book and radio series from Douglas Adams.)

Imagine the possibilities! A United Nations meeting without translator delay. Or a single contact center agent who takes calls from anyone, anywhere. In this not-so-distant future, your team can route interactions solely based on an agent's skillset, not their fluency in a specific language.

Vendors are already using AI translation for text-based chat. As the cost of real-time translation technology drops over the next several years, more vendors will offer voice solutions as part of their core platforms. To prepare to reap these and yet-unforeseen benefits of AI advancement, look for a vendor with a clear AI strategy and a verifiable record of investing in practical AI solutions.

It's not enough to say you're into AI. You need a technology partner committed to bringing AI-powered solutions to market in an actionable way. Ask the vendor about the AI products or solutions its customers are currently using, the results they've experienced, and how the vendor has adapted its strategy based on early customer feedback. That final indicator will tell you about a vendor's willingness to change. The philosophy of "die with the lie" might have worked for Will Smith's con-artist character in *Focus*, but you don't need to board a ship unwilling to adapt to your feedback.

AI is a moving target. New opportunities will appear as machine learning algorithms change and new ones emerge. Set up for success by choosing a contact center partner that thrives in a rapidly changing environment. Success with AI will result from working with a company with diversity and flexibility in their culture. In the end, it's the people that make it possible.

Automation

IVAs are an excellent example of the automation that often comes with AI. In the most sophisticated implementations, leveraging natural language processing, IVAs can automate even more inbound interactions. Remember, when dealing with people, automation isn't always *Field of Dreams* simple: You have to do more than build it for them to come.

Think about the last time you went to the airport. Did you use a kiosk to check your suitcase? Or did you go to an agent? For me, the decision between automation and human connection has more to do with the experience than the outcome. Can I check my bag using a kiosk 100% of the time? Yup. Do I? Not even half the time.

I go to a human agent whenever there are fewer than three people in line. (I used to fly a lot; the high-status line is usually pretty short.) Whether I spoke to a human or engaged with the kiosk was, essentially, a coin toss. How disappointing would that sentence be for an American Airlines automation engineer to read? But it's true.

The kiosk asks a long series of questions that aren't relevant to my situation that a human agent doesn't have to. "Are you checking golf clubs?" People can see that I am not and don't have to ask. Maybe it's a quirk of my personality, but I'd rather wait in a short line than answer the same five irrelevant questions every time I fly.

This illustrates the difference between using natural language and guided speech in your IVA implementations. If instead the kiosk asked: "What kinds of bags are you checking today?" and allowed me to answer the question freely, I might feel differently. But there are always tradeoffs. Implementing true say-anything IVAs can get expensive. And perhaps that investment isn't worth the incremental improvement in customer containment rates. It's cheaper to serve customers like me the old-fashioned way.

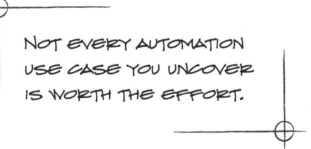

NOT EVERY AUTOMATION USE CASE YOU UNCOVER IS WORTH THE EFFORT.

Seek the same kind of balance as you approach automation. Not every automation use case you uncover is worth the effort.

Natural language IVAs might not be either. But look for options. Letting customers tell you what they want in their own words — instead of vomiting an automated list at them — will sometimes be crucial to driving adoption of your automation efforts.

Inspired by a physicist-written — so you know you can trust the math — webcomic titled *Is it Worth the Time?*[37], I always do a little math before I plunge into an automation project. Since customer expectations (and supporting technology) change so quickly, I recommend calculating the amount of time — and by extension dollars — you can spend auto-mating a project based on a three-year ROI.

To simplify this calculation for you, consider the following table:

	50/day	20/day	5/day	Daily	Weekly	Monthly
1 second	2 months	25 days	6 days	1 day	4 hours	1 hour
5 seconds	10 months	4 months	1 month	6 days	21 hours	5 hours

Figure 8-1 —How much time you can spend on automation before you spend more time than you save.

Check out that return on a 30-second gain! Whoa. You know what an agent does 50 times a day that takes 30 seconds? Typing up after-call notes — and it won't take you five years to automate either.

Your calculations will obviously require you to include the cost of the resources, but the spirit of the math is the same. Figure out how much you'll save by automating or accelerating a task. Then calculate the likely adoption rate for that automation. Finally, try to identify any hidden soft-cost savings associated with automat-ing it anyway — like time previously lost to icing the headaches employees developed from repeatedly smacking their heads against the wall.

For example, say you're considering the purchase of a workflow automation application to eliminate the need for agents to send

---

[37] https://xkcd.com/1205/

follow-up text messages once a process completes. Currently the steps go something like:

- Agent hangs up the phone.
- Agent enters notes into a case/ticket.
- Another employee performs the task, such as approving an exception, sending a service technician, or confirming an appointment.
- That person signals that they've completed the task by closing the case, emailing the agent, etc.
- The agent, as the designated customer liaison, calls or texts the customer with the good news.

It might only take a few seconds for the agent to execute step 5, and they might do it only occasionally. Even with 100 or 1,000 agents, the cost benefit of automating the task might not add up on paper. But if it's a task that agents universally hate to do and makes them consider looking for another job — then it's worth automating.

My husband owns two telescoping poles for window washing. Does he have an assistant who helps him clean the windows or extra arms that he unveils like a window-cleaning superhero cousin of Avalokiteshvara[38]? I wish. No, he has two because he doesn't like switching the squeegee out for the rag attachment on a single pole. I've watched him clean the windows many times and I can say confidently that the hassle of the quick release doesn't justify having more stuff in the utility room. For me. For him, it's a condition of the chore. My point: Automate what

---

[38] Avalokiteshvara, often depicted as having many heads and arms, is the bodhisattva of compassion in the school of Buddhism practiced in Tibet.

you need to automate to get your windows clean and keep your employees happy.

When selecting a contact center solution, look for the flexibility to automate several task types. For example, look at tasks that can help you increase customer self-service containment, reduce agent workload, automate quality assurance programs, and streamline the adds, moves, and changes of day-to-day administration.

Avoid getting caught up in one area by asking for automation examples for each persona who intends to use the solution: customer, agent, supervisor, administrator, developer. If the vendor has a mature solution, it will have example use cases to show how automation makes work easier for each of them.

Analytics

While often grouped, reporting and analytics are not the same. Traditionally, both people and systems provided the reporting, but people, exclusively, performed the analysis. First you needed a report, then you could analyze it. Today, applications can perform the analysis on your behalf. A good analytics tool will answer questions you never even considered asking. It will uncover ideas that can reshape the way your company does business, both inside and beyond the contact center.

For example, imagine you're a clothing retailer. Your contact center primarily offers order support. And via thoughtful integrations between the e-commerce, order fulfillment, and contact center solutions, your teams have achieved excellent self-service containment and automated several manual processes. Agents process mostly "highbrow" interactions — thought-requiring opportunities to delight customers.

Then one day someone calls in about trouble with a sock purchase. Then another. And another. Each caller routes to a different agent, which means no single person has the perspective to detect this trend.

But your analytics engine does.

The system elevates the sudden spike in the phrase "green socks" to supervisors who, upon further investigation, identify the issue: Green socks are being shipped with two left socks. (Socks can totally have handedness.) Sure, for the contact center, this insight allowed the supervisor to push a field alert to her team — an excellent, typical use case. But the real business value came from what the supervisor did next.

At the recommendation of her IT comrades, the supervisor emailed the order fulfillment department. That team temporarily stopped shipping green socks while it identified the batches of trouble socks. Taking it one step further, with this insight, the packaging department realized it had also packed a pallet with pairs of two right socks. Thanks to analytics, they pulled the pallet of mismatched socks before they doubled the scope of the issue.

Contact center analytics add value beyond the contact center itself. They can uncover the customer usage patterns your product and marketing teams long for, resolve logistics issues before they come to a head, and might even reveal insights sales can use to blow out revenue goals.

As the technical conscience of the business, it's your responsibility to help the contact center team choose a solution that will benefit the business as much as it will resolve its localized challenges. Look for a vendor with a flexible analytics model that:

- Enables users to explore the data to uncover the reasons behind the insights
- Surfaces topics and trends for you
- Allows you to compare or identify trends against two or more relevant-to-your-business categories

And choose one that makes the whole experience easier for business users. (We don't want them calling IT all the time, now do we?)

AI Administration

Fueled by my unbridled frugality and faced with $16/glass neighborhood juice joints, my husband and I bought a juicer five years ago. I reckoned that if I could make juice at home, we could avoid the $3 upcharge for 30 cents worth of ginger. We even selected an appliance that was a little nicer than we needed to accommodate potential vegetable scope creep. In only 20 uses this kitchen appliance would pay for itself.

Except... it's a total bitch to clean.

My apologies for the colorful language. There simply isn't any other way to put it. Cleaning the machine takes more time than the washing, chopping, juicing, and drinking... combined! Talk about the juice not being worth the squeeze.

My husband (the lone member of our household's dishwashing team) hates it when that appliance makes its way on to the counter. The juicer angst has made him skeptical of beets. Beets. I can't even look at them at the grocery store without him sighing and (not so) secretly hoping I don't plan to juice them.

But the juice is delicious. Fresh, flavorful, and worth it in my opinion. Not his.

Until recently you could say the same thing about implementing and administrating AI solutions. Their juice wasn't worth the squeeze. Not to say that the AI didn't work or that it didn't provide business value. It's simply that the effort put forth to maintain it either took too long or created an uncomfortable codependency with the solution provider.

To avoid this trap, consider three things during your contact center selection process:

- Could your line-of-business partners administer the application themselves?
- How do you train the AI model — who does it and in what application?
- What is the vendor's plan for, and philosophy toward, AI administration over the next one, two, and five years?

The answers can help you to determine whether your vendor will make a great juicer that makes your team contemplate launching it off a balcony every time they use it. Or is it creating an experience that — more expensive or not — will leave you with the time and resources necessary to run the business.

Pay special attention to the first point: Can the business team do it themselves? Training the model is part of the challenge of AI solutions. At some point someone has to review what the AI "thought," compare it to the actual customer conversation, and decide whether the AI understood it properly. Does your team really want to read or listen to call center interactions? And does your team have the contextual perspective necessary to determine customer intent based on a phrase?

Effectively democratizing AI — the idea that, if we make it simple enough, we can bring AI to the people — takes more than simply providing back-end access to the system. The industry needs to goof-proof the mechanics of managing, training, and administrating AI. We can't expect contact center staff to moonlight as language scientists. They shouldn't have to understand how machine learning models work. And they don't need to earn a degree in computer science. Come to think of it, neither should IT.

Look for a partner that is investing to bring the technology to the end user, instead of the other way around. Evaluate the user experiences they use today, ask about their future vision in that arena, and confirm that their philosophy aligns with your business's strategic AI direction.

Thanks to in-home smart devices, people think AI should "just work." But you and I know that those kinds of frictionless experiences take a lot of work, research, planning, and training — both of the AI model and of the end customers who drive the success through adoption. Make sure the juice is worth the squeeze.

MAKE SURE THE JUICE
IS WORTH THE SQUEEZE.

Supporting Developers

Despite sporting a master's degree in computer science, I consider myself a terrible programmer. It's not that I can't write good code, I just don't. I don't mean that I write bad code on purpose. I write bad code because I don't write much code. I'm probably four languages behind what's "hip," and I'm totally okay with it because I've spent the last 15 years sitting on the fence between sales and marketing.

As a sales engineer, I'd occasionally write a little code to make a demo look cool. And as a technical marketer, I occasionally develop cutesy stuff to help the product shine. But it's not my day-to-day gig, and I'm grateful for that.

I'm also grateful for solutions that make my development life easier on those rare occasions when I must dip my toe back in. I imagine it's similar for the members of your IT team. Are they tapped to deliver solutions to departments on a rotating basis, which prevents them from maintaining expertise on any specific solution? Even if your team members have historically had the luxury to dedicate focus to a single project or technology, the cloud will change that. Cloud solutions typically don't need the kinds of hands-on development their on-premises ancestors did.

Whatever the situation, your development teams want concise, clear, and complete access to developer tools like documentation, code examples, SDKs, and sandboxes. If your chosen platform has APIs (it better!), your team needs developer support. As it's unlikely someone will literally provide tech support for code they didn't write, you should expect the tools to support yourselves. Also ensure the SLAs for the platform include API availability.

PROCESS PIONEERS

Greta Stops Partying Like It's 1999

Greta is an IT supervisor who was recently promoted at an international vacuum retailer. Having been charged with bringing her department into the 21st century, she dove in headfirst.

Greta: Listen, I love the 1990s. And I love that everything from the '90s is now getting rebooted and really tugging on those nostalgia heartstrings. What I don't love is '90s dinosaur technology hanging around in the workplace long after it's been uninvited from the party.

My company develops state-of-the-art cleaning technology that once seemed like something from The Jetsons but is now an everyday part of the average household cleaning routine. So why was I, an IT supervisor, still working with systems developed before I could walk?

We have 2,500 employees and contact center agents in four international locations. When I originally joined my team as a coordinator seven years ago, we had already outgrown our previous on-premises technology. Reporting was difficult, configurations were challenging for IT, and we didn't have integration with other systems. It was challenging to script IVRs, and we couldn't route calls like we wanted. The innovation just simply wasn't there. We were leaving our customers in those endless IVR loops of "press 1 for this vague problem, press 2 for something else that will ultimately take you back to 1."

Another moment that really solidified the need to prioritize our move was when we had a service disruption every single day for the month of August. Some were quick, a few lasted hours, and it always felt like the sky was falling. My team was exhausted and always in reaction mode. I wanted them to have time to be proactive about problem solving. It was clearly time for a change. But while we had approval to review other solutions, it would take time. With a company that has such a storied legacy, it was important to handle any change with care and purpose.

I spent more than a year planning the move to the cloud with my team and heard pitches from multiple vendors. The one we chose was always the clear winner no matter which way you sliced it. We were able to undergo a major digital transformation, moving our four contact centers to the cloud and introducing additional capabilities. We could deploy new features on day one. The integrations allow our shiny new IVA to detect a known customer, pull up the record from Oracle CRM, and, if the customer owns one of the mobile-connected products, automatically route the call to the team that handles those products. If there is a wait, the IVA provides the predicted time and offers the customer the option to receive a callback.

We've had agents tell us that they call our new software "The Wizard." The blended outbound dialing capabilities have kept agents busy and managing callback queues. In fact, our agent occupancy is now so solidly in the "green zone" that supervisors no longer have to worry about managing agent time. Because we trust the system to keep everyone busy, we can trust people to work where we can't watch. We gave 80% of our customer service workforce the option to work remotely. This helps us compete in today's employment market and really position ourselves as a leader in cleaning tech because our support tech is so strong.

Since moving to the cloud, we have experienced a 9% increase in customer satisfaction scores measured over thousands of interactions. Again, none of this data would have been available using our old tech. And if it were, I sure couldn't figure out how to view it.

AI and automation is now our gold standard — and the norm. Our customers receive answers in a natural, conversational way without speaking to a live agent. We've scaled service without compromising quality. At the end of the day, our customers just want to be treated with kindness and get a sense that we'll have a solution when they ask for help. And now, I feel confident that we can deliver that feeling every day.

CHAPTER NINE

MAKING IT A HOME

What makes a home a home? Setting aside the existential responses like "home is where the heart is," think about the things realtors remove to stage a house for sale. They take out all the personal items — the photos, tchotchkes, and throw pillows — that make the home uniquely yours. Right now, your contact center looks like a house staged for sale. As the new homeowners, you can begin to invite the teams to imagine how they will transform it into a home.

Personalization by Business Unit/Location

One of my first jobs in software was working for a, roughly, 40-person startup in Chicago. It was the last job I had where I worked from an actual office. Our team created a "support fort." We took down the walls between our cubes and — because we had nowhere else to place them — leaned them against the perimeter. It made the area look like a fort, so naturally, we hung a flag. It made it fun and allowed us to feel like masters of our domain.

By now I trust you've embraced the importance of letting your business partners weigh in on the fit of the solution. I'm confident they already have ideas regarding the flags they want to fly. Now's the time to make it happen. Team by team, the implementation can roll out the figurative red carpets. The individualization capabilities you'll want to consider include:

- Differing compliance needs (PCI, HIPAA, etc.)
- Customizable hours of operation
- Different "follow-the-sun" philosophies
- Billing back telephony charges to the department
- Bespoke integration needs (niche CRMs, for example)
- Unique needs for agent enablement and interaction memorialization

Adoption

Anyone who's raised kids knows that filling the room with their personal items engenders a sense of ownership. It's their space. Children, like adults, are more likely to want to spend time in, and maintain, a space that's uniquely theirs.

SaaS vendors depend on solution stickiness. Many don't even turn a profit until year two. So, they really want to make sure you adopt their solution. As IT, you have that in common. Can you imagine the headache if a solution didn't work and the business wanted to change it every couple years? Yikes!

Luckily, software vendors have invested in flexibility and self-service to ensure adoption. Choose a solution that maximizes options for individuals to personalize their workspaces. Can agents create an avatar? Can supervisors customize dashboards? Reports? Can the team turn off or hide irrelevant features?

Ultimately end-user adoption stems from three components:

- Does the tool do what I need it to do?
- Do I feel empowered (vs. constrained) while using it?
- Do I like using it?

Don't underestimate the power of the third component. I've personally rescued several companies from a competitor's product simply because the users didn't like using it. They didn't feel like it was "theirs." And they were unhappy with how the decision was made. Now, that wasn't the reason presented to justify changing solutions. They came to us with a whole host of things that "didn't work right." But if I'm being honest, the solution I represented did things pretty much the exact same way.

It really came down to the fact that the business didn't like that IT made the choice for them. Like a child that walks past a toy Mom holds to choose a less cool one from the toy store shelf, my customers found nits to pick with IT's choice so they could take back the power they felt they had lost.

Good for me, bad for IT.

Ownership

People like things they control. It's human nature. Some people are more intent on controlling things than others, but that's just personality. But if you think about why people still buy books when the library is right around the corner, you'll get answers like "I want to read it whenever I want" or "I like to write in the margins." Not that these aren't fine justifications, but when you get down to it, they are just excuses to control the situation — access or utility.

To further drive adoption, IT should deposit as much of the ownership responsibility back onto the business units that utilize the tool the most. Empower them to make their own adds, moves, and changes. Provide or encourage training. Share data impact diagrams to help them understand where else contact center data flows. Encourage them to own their change initiatives — with you acting as a guide.

Partner Solutions

As the contact center team matures its implementation, it may find benefit from a partner solution that's pre-integrated to work with the core platform. A robust contact center platform won't require a myriad of partner products to assemble a complete solution. But don't expect to solve every challenge with the same platform.

Think of it this way: You might buy the 20-piece cookware set. It's great. It even came with one of those pasta-steamer-strainer combination pots. Just because your partner also loves French breakfasts and demands a crepe pan doesn't mean the cookware set is bad or incomplete. Most people don't make crepes, so it doesn't make sense for the company to bundle that in. In fact, the specialized nature of the materials in a quality crepe pan might vary enough from the typical cookware manufacturing process that the company chose to partner with a company specializing in crepe pans. Applaud that choice. Not only did the company acknowledge that someone else does it better, but it also found that company to make it easy for you to access the specialized cookware you need.

Or maybe you had no idea your partner would get into crepes when you purchased your pans. They never mentioned crepes before. Who knows what the future holds? Especially in the rapidly changing environment of customer-driven contact center requirements, it's hard to predict what specialized solutions you'll need in the future.

You can prepare your company for success by choosing a contact center vendor that understands and acknowledges its limitations and has a robust and expanding ecosystem of partner solutions at the ready.

Go Beyond APIs, Step into the Voice Stream

While we're on the topic of partner solutions, there's a component of some contact center platforms that can affect your ability to utilize recent advancements in AI and automation. Specifically, real-time access to the voice stream — the literal stream of audio data generated during a conversation — is vital if you want to provide live coaching. Many solutions offer some form of this out of the box, but industry leaders also make it easy for third parties to access the data.

Real-time access to the voice stream allows leading AI-powered solution providers to partner and integrate with your vendor's solution and deliver capabilities like soft-skill coaching, tone correction, live call translation, and overall better agent assistance.

Single Contract

You may be inclined to demand that all the providers wrap their solutions into a single contact. Having it all on the "same paper" means fewer legal reviews, streamlined renewals, and a single point of contact when you need something. But don't let the mild inconvenience of managing multiple vendors stand in the way of a great solution.

Some tools bill using consumption models, while others employ per-user licensing. It simply might not make financial sense for you, or the providers in question, to consolidate onto a single contract or bill. That said, you know such demands are up for negotiation if you're a large enterprise. Every vendor I've ever worked with would find a way to make it happen, for the right deal. Just consider what benefits your business more in the long run: a beefier SLA or a single contract? You have only so many chips to play; use them wisely.

PROCESS PIONEERS

Tim Sees the Forest and the Trees

Tim is the Global IT Director for a large hospitality software and solutions provider. Recently promoted from a regional role, he found himself overseeing a vast department that had undergone a recent data migration that caused difficulties implementing the new cloud call center solutions equally across all regions.

Tim: I took over for my boss when he retired. On his way out the door, he told me, "A captain always goes down with his ship, unless he is smart enough to retire first." Comforting, I thought, as I was about to take the helm.

I oversee multiple international contact center locations for a global hospitality software company. We recently decided to move everything to the cloud to unify the customer service experience. I was thrilled, as I'd previously struggled to maintain the US and Canadian on-premises call centers. Now, covering all global territories, I couldn't imagine doing it without a cloud migration.

Unfortunately, it was only about three months into the migration when my VP and I realized we had chosen the wrong cloud provider. It seemed everything was going wrong. We'd been so focused on getting our entire company onto one platform that we didn't consider that our regional call centers used different processes. Not every region could work with our one-size-fits-all solution and our provider couldn't customize even the smallest things to simplify things for our agents.

We began receiving a variety of complaints from sales managers. When we tried to address them, the vendor didn't have a solution to offer. These were seemingly simple things like sales agents in a country with stringent compliance laws needed their call logs integrated with their government's do not call list service. Our vendor could provide one integration to a government database. One! Last time I checked, there were hundreds of governments out there. It's not like we can pick just one.

Our Asia territories marketing department had a strong need for soft-skills training, but marketing in many Asian markets is incredibly different than other parts of the globe. We had a great feature to layer in an AI tool to do real-time sentiment analysis and coaching, but we couldn't customize it for each region.

We also never received good services from them for support, configuration, or customization, despite having assurances in numerous meetings with the vendor's executives. Again, we hold some blame for not doing due diligence before diving in. Lesson learned.

As the center of operations, our contact center provides 24x7 support to ensure that our customers' hospitality brands can deliver excellence to their guests. We didn't think it was out of the question to ask the same of our software solutions company.

Meanwhile, I quietly began researching some alternative providers, which is how I discovered our new vendor. It had impressive support and customization options — and countless customer accounts to back it up! I knew I'd get blowback for suggesting another migration so soon, but I had to do it. Ignoring the small details would eventually eat at us from the inside and cause huge financial trouble.

Fortunately, my colleagues agreed. We initiated the migration with as little stress as possible. People were not-so-secretly thrilled that we replaced our last provider. And our new vendor re-energized us.

Now we have integrations that suit each individual call center, all supported by one provider. It's nice to have the flexibility to purchase additional functionality and plug it only into the areas of the business that need it. I learned a valuable lesson: Being a good leader means knowing when to take a step back and look at the forest and when to dive in and admire the trees!

CHAPTER TEN

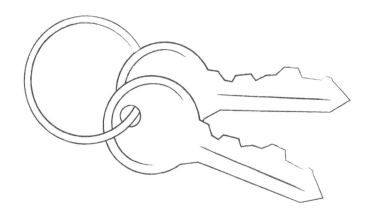

TAKING A FINAL WALKTHROUGH

My favorite part of buying a new house is that moment on the way to the closing when you take one last look before the broker hands you the keys. Your new place is clean and ready for your fresh start. All the hard work — the research, negotiation, and waiting — is behind you. You can relax because you're, quite literally, about to get on with your life.

At this phase of the implementation, IT can begin to unwind from the project.

Training

Training at this phase should be at least partially tailored to your specific implementation. Encourage the team to take the time to learn the application before moving into user acceptance testing (UAT). I'd argue the best time to complete training is concurrent with the discovery phase of the implementation. My most successful customers are those who "learned the LEGOs" before the implementation went into full swing. This allowed them to adapt their vision and expectations to the platform. Regardless of when you decide to train your team, you have a few decisions to make regarding format.

In-Person vs. Online

Different people learn differently. In a post-COVID climate, more people have developed the skills necessary to learn online and fewer desire in-person training. Consequently, many vendors have been slow to return to onsite training models as their primary offering. But if your implementation is large enough, it may make sense to pursue hands-on training for your power users, especially administrators in the business units and IT. In-person trainings tend to have more breadth, encourage deeper questions, and yield better results due to the increased focus of attendees.

Online trainings, on the other hand, scale well. They allow you to train more people, and when recorded, more often. Choose online trainings if your use cases are commonplace, you experience frequent turnover, or want to educate additional employees for whom contact center might not be their primary focus.

In either case, expect a "train the trainer" model in which the vendor trains administrators and supervisors, but not individual agents. Due to the typically high agent turnover in contact centers, it's more economical to focus on training the leadership team. That way they can incorporate agent platform training into the training for ramping new agents.

University On Demand

On-demand trainings for all elements of the solution is a must. Even if your team completed instructor-led trainings, you want an on-demand option. In the online university scenario, your team can access the latest training as CCaaS solutions frequently add functionality. People have the flexibility to review content as they need it. Maybe it's something they forgot because they don't use every feature every day. Or you're bringing new team members up to speed quickly since not every hire will coincide with or justify an instructor-led course. On-demand courses also serve as the primary mechanism for training agents.

Look for vendors that offer all three training options and have completion exams or certifications. These both signal maturity in the content and offer a resume item that will benefit agents and managers alike.

User Acceptance Testing

IT's role in UAT for contact center solutions is typically light since your team isn't the primary end user. (Unless you've been so inspired that you decided to deploy it for an IT helpdesk: a very strong use case for contact center solutions.)

While the vendor or implementation partner likely performed most of the heavy lifting, your department should still spot check the integrations and telephony components.

Integration Testing

Back in the support fort in Chicago, I was asked to integrate our startup's application with Salesforce — in my spare time. I was fresh out of school and eager to impress, so I whipped together an integration between support calls. In hindsight, I should have asked more questions up front. I didn't realize we subscribed to a version of Salesforce with a very limited API usage allowance. I used up our whole API quota — during testing. We found out when the bill for the overages came after our go-live. Oops.

Companies are less stingy with their API allocations these days. And companies that charge by call are very transparent about pricing. But it's worth examining the load that any integrations requested by the line-of-business teams put on your other applications. just in case.

Telephony Testing

From the telephony side, this is an ideal time to set up all your functional and planned testing. For instance:

- Map all the call trees.
- Identify the test users, regions, and phone numbers.
- Set up alerts and establish plans for any surfaced failures.
- Write or update your disaster recovery plans to reflect the new system.
- Use test numbers to verify the customer experience.
- Perhaps even solicit opinions from the marketing team to ensure the new application is on-brand.

Many vendors offer testing services or applications to automate functional and ongoing testing. These tools are pre-integrated to the platforms and go by names from on-the-nose enterprise testing suite to clever like Razor (a subtle reference to the simple solutions offered by the Occam's razor parable).

If you don't have an in-house solution from your existing contact center, I highly recommend investing in a testing solution. They function as an insurance policy for your investment. By testing that your lines are up, the IVAs are operational, and the APIs are responding as expected, you protect your investment and can act upon any issues before they impact revenue or other areas of the business.

Utilizing an automatic testing service is particularly important if you:

- Brought your own carrier
- Utilize telephony services in regions with less-developed telephony infrastructure
- Have complex IVAs or phone trees
- Depend on third-party integrations, especially for revenue-impacting use cases like payment processing or appointment scheduling

- Change prompts frequently based on events like holidays or promotions
- Want to avoid human error
- Care about preserving the brand
- Don't have time or resources to test manually

PROCESS PIONEERS

How Callie Crushed UAT

Callie works for a company that ships industrial-grade restaurant kitchen supplies worldwide. She worked closely with her business partners in the contact center and the vendor to design a comprehensive UAT plan.

Callie: As a single parent of three teen boys, there's no greater crisis than a problem in the kitchen. To them, any delay with a meal hitting the table is about as catastrophic as a pimple on prom night. At work, the smallest delay on our end could mean missed meals somewhere. I wouldn't wish that on anyone.

When it came time to do UAT for our new contact center, I couldn't leave anything to chance. My first major task was to ensure our team was ready. Fortunately, our vendor provided simple instructions to distribute to my team. Making sure everyone's headsets were operational and everyone knew the basics of the intuitive platform was easy. You never want to get too comfortable when going into a major launch, but everything was looking great!

Still, when your company is constantly moving huge products and parts internationally, you want to be sure you have reliable help 24x7. You know, in case the six dozen stoves you sent to a major European hotel don't arrive and the manager has someone to call when 15 walk-in freezers show up instead.

The second part of testing was to verify that the actual phone lines worked. This would require a lot of hours of trial and error identifying the cracks in our armor before going live. We had only a limited window before launch, and I worried we might not meet our deadline with the stability our customers deserve.

Two big problems were a big reason for deploying the new system: call abandonment and call disconnection rates. Due to our high volume of clients from more than 20 countries, we would regularly have to triage things as issues popped up. Sometimes people would hang up due to long hold times, then call back frustrated an hour later. This, of course, led to a steep decline in customer satisfaction. Other times, lines would just drop. But it was difficult to tell the two scenarios apart on our old application.

I knew that switching to a new contact center would be the key to assisting our customers in a timely and reliable manner. We'd have to test all the lines to make sure they were operational in each country. Then I needed to measure which were bailing and design a way to prevent hang-ups so our customers could get dinners on plates for their customers.

One night, I was helping my youngest son with his homework when I had an idea that could solve all my problems. He asked me to review an essay he was writing to make sure it made sense. "Do you want me to proof-read for errors?" I asked. He shook his head. "No, bots do all that now." Jamie showed me a site where AI combs through your essays for grammar and spelling errors. It made spell-check's red squiggles look as obsolete as a rotary telephone.

I scoffed at my kid. Surely, he knew that a good pair of human eyes is no match for a linguistic algorithm. "You never miss a typo that's right in front of you because you've already read something 10 times?" he asked. That's exactly what was stressing me about our UAT. We had been in the trenches so long, going over the same potential issues, that I worried whether there were issues that we could no longer see. This might be a job for the robots after all.

We decided to splurge on an automated testing suite. The kid was right: Sometimes AI is better than the diminishing returns of a tired human. The software more than paid for itself, especially when it came time to verify the flawless processing of international calls and messages. It dramatically reduced the time crunch of our final pre-launch testing and gave us confidence we needed in the home stretch.

Thanks to our rock-solid UAT we launched without a hitch! The automated testing was so helpful that we decided to keep it permanently to make sure our phone lines and virtual assistants would always be up and running. There's nothing like a good insurance policy to provide peace of mind. Our call abandonment rate (which, it turns out, was mostly the result of calls involuntarily disconnecting) dropped dramatically in the first month, which meant significantly happier customers. More importantly, it meant less downtime and less potential revenue lost from kitchens.

I went home on launch day knowing that our customers had an easy and reliable way to talk to someone about any issues immediately. Jamie asked what I was cooking for dinner. I asked if he wanted to do some UAT on the pasta sauce. There are still some jobs you can't leave to a robot.

CHAPTER ELEVEN

MOVING DAY!

What an exciting moment it is to see all your hard work pay off and watch the team take their first interactions — digital and audio — on the new platform. Order some pizza (or grab a bag of oranges) and celebrate. If you've shared and followed the advice I've laid out so far, moving day will be as simple as flipping on a light switch.

But just to make sure it all goes right, let's talk about the service and support elements that make it happen.

Go-Live

The best go-lives are boring. But that doesn't mean they shouldn't be well-supervised. Expect the vendor (or partner) implementation team to offer resources for launch day to verify everything goes smoothly and to swarm on any issues that do arise. If you have a location with a large team of agents, it's reasonable to request on-site support. The billed-back cost of travel is more than covered by the peace of mind and rapid response to anything that arises while the team gets their sea legs.

Telephony Cutovers

The days of splitting traffic and soft launches are behind us. Expect a hard cut for specific business units rather than diverting a percentage of traffic. Assuming you plan to use the new vendor as your telephony carrier, a best practice for handling these hard cutover events is to:

- Apply for a RespOrg[39] transfer to the new vendor (months before you need it).
- Set up temporary numbers for each customer experience.
- On the day of, temporarily forward all the numbers to the temporary numbers.

That way when the RespOrg executes, even if it's not at the precise time of your go-live (as is often true), all traffic will flow to the new system via the forward until it flows there directly after the RespOrg transfer kicks in.

If you're bringing your own carrier, the process is a little different. First you will work with the vendor to establish the necessary SIP trunks to your existing carrier. Then, on game day, you simply move the numbers from the current trunk group to the new one with your new contact center vendor. Easy peasy.

Timing the Event

Most call centers have fewer calls mid to late week, so Wednesdays and Thursdays may be an ideal time to go-live. One last thought on end user training: Don't train too early.

---

[39] The RespOrg, or responsible organization, is the company that maintains the registration for toll-free phone numbers on the North American Numbering Plan. Basically, your numbers' carrier.

Agent trainings probably contain less than a day of content. I recommend training no more than three days before go-live (but ideally two). That leaves one day for information to sink in and for the team to ask questions, but it's not so long that they forget what they learned before getting a chance to apply it in real life.

PROCESS PIONEERS

For Simone, Anticipation Is Like a Box of Chocolates

Simone is a business school graduate with over a dozen years of experience in the hospitality industry. A national hotel chain hired her to implement a new cloud-based customer support call center; her go-live wasn't lacking in hospitality.

Simone: I anxiously looked over at the clock that morning: 27 minutes to go. If everything goes smoothly, this launch will take my team into the stratosphere. One minor miscalculation? I'd be facing an unmitigated disaster — on a national scale. I'm in charge of a major hotel chain's customer support services, and today is the go-live for our new call center.

For someone who works at a business that guarantees a good night's sleep, I was up late, tossing and turning, thinking of all the things that could go wrong. What if the call center isn't online right away? What if the customer who waited endlessly on hold for help has a business account with 100 reservations a week? Or, just as bad, what if it's a family of four waiting at the front desk after a 12-hour travel day wondering what happened to the adjoining rooms they've been looking forward to for 2,000 miles?

Our history with customer support was anything but a five-star experience. We originally tried to house our contact center at our corporate headquarters. But with customers traveling and arriving at all hours of the day and night, there were inevitably issues that needed attention around the clock. Keeping one call center staffed 24 hours a day turned out to be more than we could handle. So, like many businesses, we turned to the cloud for help. We got a storm instead.

We switched to a cloud-based system during peak summer travel in anticipation of our annual high volume of guests looking to ditch their luggage quickly and hit the pool. It was 4th of July weekend, but the real fireworks were from angry guests who found themselves on hold for over an hour. By the time people finally got through, issues with their reservation were only part of their complaint: They were just as frustrated with the miserable wait and wondering how any business of our size would leave a guest waiting on the line long enough to watch three episodes of Seinfeld.

Now, as the person brought on to clean up the embarrassing mess left by my predecessor, the stakes couldn't be higher for today's launch. It wasn't just my reputation on the line, but that of our company. You can have the world's greatest property, but rooms will stay empty if people don't feel cared for. And there's nothing hospitable about leaving someone looking for help stranded with a 45-second loop of hold music.

I was feeling too uneasy to eat a proper breakfast and instead opted for a cup of our hotel's signature lobby coffee and a bowl of the little chocolates that we leave on pillows. I'm not sure why I thought caffeine and chocolate would ease my last-minute jitters. Then, with three minutes to go, I got a notification from my vendor contact asking if I could hop on a quick video chat.

A quick chat? What could be wrong? I meticulously followed all their instructions, prepped everyone on my team, then double-checked all the work. Then I triple-checked it. I held my breath, braced for the worst, and opened the chat window.

He greeted me with a smile and couldn't help but chuckle at the evident panic in my eyes. "Relax!" he said. "It's not bad. Maybe I should've mentioned that." He had sent a special delivery for launch day, but the courier was having trouble finding my office. I sighed with relief and told him how nervous I was for this go-live.

"The goal is boring," he said. "If this is the most boring and uneventful go-live in history, then we've done our job." Then he looked at his watch. "Look at that! We've already been live for 10 seconds. Feels boring on my end. What about you?" I looked around my empty office. No emails from frantic employees or angry customers. No phones ringing off the hook from corporate. Just a deep unremarkable silence.

Until... KNOCK! KNOCK! I knew there was a courier on the way, but I still jumped. The courier apologized for being late and explained that the store gave them the wrong address. "I tried calling them, but they put me on hold for 20 minutes. Can you imagine?"

I sat back at my desk, soaking in the uneventful silence of a job well done, and unwrapped the launch gift. It was a giant box of chocolates. I took it to the break room to share, then realized I was finally comfortable enough to eat a real breakfast.

Day 2 Support

All right, go-live went without a hitch and the team is doing its thing delighting customers. Now what? Who do they call when they need help? You, internal IT? The vendor? The implementation partner? Making assumptions about support roles and responsibilities during purchase can create confusion and disappointment, so let's spell out some best practices to follow and properly define everyone's role.

Agent Helpdesk

Who ya gonna call (when an agent has a problem)? (*Ghostbusters!*) You. Especially with distributed teams, I recommend you have individual agents call your IT department or a similar central team for initial troubleshooting. Most agent-level issues are related to the local ISP. If it were platform-wide, the vendor's monitoring would have already caught it. Your IT department is best suited to help agents troubleshoot the browser, internet connection, any VPN-like security on their machine, and headset-related issues. Rely on the vendor to provide agent-level diagnostic information for things like voice quality to help ascertain whether to escalate the issues to the vendor's support team.

If your team isn't staffed to support your individual agent base — or if you want to use this change as an opportunity to redeploy those resources — discuss options with the vendor. Many will offer advanced support services — either directly or via a partner — to accommodate your high-touch desires.

Break-Fix Support

Without a doubt, the vendor (or their resell partner) should handle break-fix support. Make sure the core package includes support for anything they've sold or built for your organization. This support should be 24x7 and offered via a portal and/or personal communication channels like email, phone, and chat. If your vendor can't support your team's omnichannel support preferences, how can you expect its product to support your business's desire to offer the same?

Consider how well a vendor appears to eat their own dog food (uses its own product). If a CRM salesperson can't seem to remember your interaction history — a principle use case for CRM

— hang up immediately and shop elsewhere. Similarly, if the contact center vendor can't deliver good support via its own product, how are you supposed to?

It's more than fair to ask to experience their support or speak with customer references during the consideration process. Do they offer support in your preferred language? In all the languages in which your teams do business? Are they helpful? What are the SLAs for different case priorities — both for initial contact and ongoing updates? Finally, obtain clarity on integration support. The particulars of the plan are less important than the fact that you need a plan.

Technical Account Management Services

Have you ever been at the gym, working out, minding your own business, when some dude in a two-sizes-too-small tank top strolls up to sell you his personal training services? The scene surely warrants the knee-jerk response, of "no, I'm good." But after a while, I started to wonder whether there might be something inherently bad about my exercise form that caused trainers to approach me and not the people working out to my left or right.

Faced with plateauing performance and seemingly chronic muscle tightness, I decided to give one a try. Pete is nice. He quickly got to know me, how I'm motivated, and how best to deliver feedback. He makes fun of me when I do things wrong. I feel silly, laugh, and remember to do it better next time. It's unorthodox, but it works.

Pete's willingness to adapt his style to mine has led to a long-lasting, successful relationship. I can now do more pull-ups than I did in high school and my back isn't constantly sore after workouts. In retrospect, he saved me time, effort, and well... pain. Had I understood the results my old techniques left on the table, I would have gladly paid him double his rate. (Don't tell Pete!)

An investment in a technical account manager (TAM) is like that of a personal trainer. A TAM is an industry expert your vendor typically offers as a service. TAMs know the ins and outs of contact centers and your industry, and they work to understand your business so they can help you maximize the ROI of your deployment. TAMs provide best practices; bring deep, continuously updated capability knowledge; help you improve operational KPIs; perform advanced solution development and project support; deliver strategic planning; and serve as a singular point of contact for escalations.

So, you might wonder: Why don't more companies use TAM services?

For the same reasons most people don't invest in personal trainers. We think we're doing fine on our own; we don't need some expensive "expert" to help. With many companies charging anywhere from $300–$600 an hour for TAM services, who can blame people for not immediately seeing the value?

Spoiler alert: TAMs are worth it.

Since the ROI looks different for average vs. very large contact centers, let's walk through the numbers for each scenario.

TAM ROI for Typical Contact Centers (100–500 Seats)

In the average-sized, small to medium business (SMB) contact center, managers typically wear a lot of hats. They do leadership work like supervising and coaching staff, driving business initiatives, and managing leading indicators of success. But they will also spend many hours chasing down support tickets, documenting and performing changes, and other very tactical work. It's a lot for one person to manage. To employ the rare someone who can toggle between strategic thinking and tactical execution without dropping any balls, SMB customers will overspend on the resource. And they don't employ just one manager, they'll hire a few.

So, for the sake of doing some math, let's assume each of those people cost $70K a year. How much would you be willing to spend to reimagine the role being filled by a much-easier-to-find, fewer-hat-wearing, $50K resource?

TAMs help by taking a load off these managers, and they do so very efficiently. By hiring a TAM for just 10 hours a month ($48K annually), you can simplify the manager job description and let people do what they do best. At a three-manager shop, that's like spending $48K to save $60K. I'll take a 25% return any day!

And that's just in staffing. Once the TAM focuses their expert lens on the business, you will surely see the ROI shoot up.

TAM ROI for Large, Enterprise Contact Centers (500–5,000 Seats)

The math from the previous section can still apply in larger contact centers, but in my experience large companies already use economies of scale to simplify job descriptions in middle management. Therefore, in large companies, the role of the TAM is a little different, a bit more strategic, and sometimes even resembling that of an insurance policy.

The bigger the contact center, the more money is on the line when something breaks or a project goes off the rails. Large enterprises, therefore, contract TAMs as project or program leaders, consultants of best practices, and advocates for support escalations. In the event of an outage or mishap, TAMs will help reduce the mean time to resolution (MTR), chase down the root cause, and help you make plans to avoid the problem in the future.

So, the ROI calculation becomes about capitalizing on opportunity costs and valuing TAMs like you'd value an insurance policy. Say the business generates or preserves X amount of revenue daily inside the contact center and any service interruption — be it from outage or mistake — will jeopardize Y% of that, how much would you spend to insure that value?

Your TAM will tailor risk mitigation strategies to fit your needs, elevate your support cases more efficiently, and get you out of harm's way faster. The reduction in MTR provides insurance against these often-significant losses. One of my customers shared that preventing even two hours of downtime equated to 5x of what it paid for TAM services annually!

TAM ROI for Contact Centers Over 5,000 Seats

As you continue to move up in agent count, the ROI for TAM services only improves. The more agents you have performing a task, the greater the impact a small or incremental improvement will make. It's the butterfly effect: Small changes in initial conditions — whether good or bad — multiplied across thousands of agents add up to huge differences on the bottom line. Your TAM will help identify opportunities to make those changes; they will bring the tweaks and oil the squeaks. They will more than pay for themselves.

Managed Services

Last year my husband and I moved back to the beach. We'd had enough of the responsibility that accompanied our single-family home and wanted a simpler life. Don't get me wrong, we are both able-bodied DIYers who spent most of the lockdown building and creating a — dare I say — legendary entertainment space. My husband even installed a support beam under the house so we could host even more people without worrying about floor sag. Between the decorative concrete wall, tile work on the bar, woodwork of the counter, lighting and electrical, and more, we developed countless skills and gained invaluable experiences. Two years, a few tears, and several splinters later we hosted friends for some epic events.

Why did we decide to hot drop it and move to the beach? Dealing with a big house, beautiful or not, wasn't our style. We want life to be relaxing, not riddled in rehab projects. Faced with an endless parade of chores and fixer-upper opportunities, and with no competent contractors in sight, we were done.

We might have stayed if our neighborhood had provided some sort of community managed services — or at least vetted providers — to take these tasks off our plate. But once we remembered that kind of luxury does exist — it's called condominium living, by the way — the house had no shot. There's something inherently delightful about walking past a dirty poolside window and knowing it's not my problem.

Managed services — the software equivalent of condo life — are a great option if your organization wants to enjoy the simplicity and focus afforded by outsourcing your daily contact center maintenance.

Vendor Provided

The advantage to using vendor-provided managed services stems from the idea that you'll keep a single point of contact. You can be confident that the vendor's employees know the product, its upgrades, and have the latest training and certifications. They work with up-to-the-minute information.

On the other hand, most SaaS companies aren't trying to build a significant portion of their revenue from managed services. Their business model and associated capitalization comes from a high-margin, quickly scalable model that can't rely on the expense of building an army of full-time consultants. Consequently, vendor-provided services tend to carry a higher price tag than those delivered by third parties.

Partner or Systems Integrator–Provided

Partner-supplied managed services have a potential trade-off related to product training and timeliness vs. the direct-from-the-vendor option. But you're in good shape if you choose a partner certified by the vendor for its support. That signals that both parties will remain committed to their mutual — and by extension, your — success.

Third-party managed services can also lend a depth of expertise from your industry that the vendor might not have in-house. System integration partners may provide the added benefit of previous experience with your organization from other consulting engagements. That perspective can prove vital if you're looking for more than adds-moves-changes — something that might resemble a hybrid outsourced administrator and consultant.

I will offer a single caution about using partners for your managed-service needs: Choose a partner with deep contact center experience. In my experience, even consultants with deep industry expertise and knowledge of your business may lack contact center excellence. Be especially careful with partners with whom your relationship is primarily built on PBXs and circuits. Contact center is a specialized use case. Hire a specialist.

> CONTACT CENTER IS A SPECIALIZED USE CASE. HIRE A SPECIALIST.

PROCESS PIONEERS

Roger Ramps a Team Quickly

The IT director for a prestigious technical college, Roger realized he would need to quickly ramp up his call center agent staff after his first year on the job.

Roger: I have friends who graduated 10 years ago who still get nightmares that they're back in college and unprepared for a final exam. As someone who is on a university campus every day, only now as the IT director, a nightmare about studying would be a welcome reprieve.

You name it and I am here to tell you it came across my desk during my first year here. I had students message me the night before graduation saying the credits they'd earned over the past four years weren't showing up in the system. I've had parents ask for access to their daughter's student portal to make sure she's keeping up with assignments. I even had an angry alum call to complain that the football team hadn't scored all season. He was fully aware he had the wrong department, but I was the only one picking up a phone on a Saturday night. Go figure.

With close to 20,000 students across nine colleges, it was clear I'd need to scale a team quickly to handle all these problems effectively. No one wants to sit on hold for 90 minutes when they're struggling to access course materials the night before a midterm. I knew that fellow students would understand most of these problems the best and deal with them most effectively. The fact that we're a university that specializes in tech added to my confidence that my team would be up to the task.

With the help of our vendor, quickly scaling teams for the IT helpdesk, and later the entire contact center, wasn't an issue. Most of our agents decided to work remotely, but we kept one contact center open on campus so students could walk in during business hours. Everything seemed to work perfectly for the first few months.

Except for a handful of minor in-house issues, we sorted tickets quickly and didn't amass a backlog of major problems. But like any IT pro can tell you, the time to panic is when it's all going smoothly. That's the moment just before everything suddenly isn't.

I got a call from one of my agents but couldn't hear him when I picked up. I waited a bit in case he was on mute, then hung up. He quickly sent a message that his headset wasn't working. When you're in the business of answering calls, that's kind of a big hiccup!

I've been in IT for some time, so one malfunctioning headset was a minor issue. We went to work trying to determine the issue before deciding if it was something for which we needed our vendor. First things first: Turn everything off and on again. Quite literally the oldest trick in the book. When that didn't work, we started troubleshooting.

Still unable to talk to the agent by phone, we typed back and forth hoping to crack the case. Our vendor provides a robust set of tools and clear troubleshooting instructions, so I was confident we would resolve the issue quickly.

Then, I got another message. A second agent reported that their headset wasn't working. Before I could reply, a third chimed in. I love to fix things when I can, but in the world of IT, I follow the same rules as I do in baseball: three strikes and the ticket is out to the vendor.

Did I scale my team too quickly? What good are a dozen agents, ready to go around the clock, if you can't hear a word they're saying? It was the middle of exam week. And I was extremely concerned about any issues students might have during late-night cram sessions.

I opened a ticket with our vendor and got a response moments later. Their network operations team had detected one-way audio issues with one of the carriers. Once the support rep realized it was impacting my contact center, they immediately started rerouting traffic to alternative carriers. What a relief to have a vendor with proactive support.

One magic press of a button and everyone was back to work. The great support center silence was over in just 17 minutes. Our vendor thanked us for notifying them of the glitch and told me not to hesitate to call directly if the issue returned.

It felt great to know that I had successfully ramped my team with enough members to handle the job, and even greater to know our vendor had a team backing us up to handle anything we couldn't. Now if I could just get our football team to score a touchdown.

CHAPTER TWELVE

HOSTING YOUR FIRST DINNER PARTY

The first time I watched the show *Mad Men*, I was impressed by two things: the functional alcoholism (lol) and the use of the dinner party to advance an agenda. The dinner parties in the show always had a purpose: impress a client, impress a neighbor, impress your boss. The only purpose of my dinner parties was to trick people into a game of Scrabble. (I'm a sucker for a good game night.)

Whether or not that's actually how things worked in the 1960s, there's a lesson here about the role positive impressions play on our ability to influence people.

Congratulations, you successfully purchased and deployed a modern contact center platform! Your business will benefit from all the agilities and efficiencies afforded by the cloud. Let's invite some friends over and celebrate.

After all, why have a beautiful, bespoke contact center forever home if you can't share it with family and friends — who, in this analogy, represent your executive leadership and related departments. We've spoken along the way about opportunities to unlock and share contact center insights with the other areas of the business. This is your opportunity to make that happen. But first we must define success. We can't humble brag over dinner if we don't have well-defined metrics and a plan to measure our progress.

PROCESS PIONEERS

Pat's Perspicacious Partnering

Pat is a young leader whose company, a US furniture retailer with more than 50 locations, recognized their talent and promoted them to CIO at the age of 27. Despite their genius and propensity for big-picture strategizing, Pat couldn't move ahead without improving their soft skills, which ultimately propelled both their and the company's trajectory.

Pat: I'm intrigued by the world and interconnectedness. Reading about and contemplating scenarios in which we harness AI to improve how we work and live is one of my pastimes. I earned my MBA in IT Management at 24 and became a CIO at 27. Despite my education and work successes, I'd never realized that my unique perspective could be valuable to others and that it only took a small initial effort to harness the power of the collective.

A few months ago, our CEO, Doug, called me into his office. "Pat! Our external advisors have helped us narrow down options for our new contact center system. I need you to decide which one is better." That was typical Doug:

laser-focused and steps ahead in the conversation but expecting an immediate reply.

We'd talked about updating our communications infrastructure, but I wasn't aware that he'd been discussing specific solutions. "What are we looking at?" I asked. "How do the options align with our five-year business goals?"

Doug looked bewildered, which was rare. "Five-year goals? You said our phone lines were stifling our customer experience potential and growth. Now I'm giving you a choice of two of the best software solutions on the market."

Although Doug expected me to sit in his office until I picked one, I convinced him to give me a few days to explore the options. He wasn't happy about the delay, but he trusted my choices. Until then, he had relied on me for all things IT in a straight-forward manner that involved me selling him on the solution I chose. My question about the five-year goals threw him off, not only because I was seeking his input, but it suggested that the shiniest product wouldn't guarantee success.

Doug likes quick and efficient solutions, especially with lots of bells and whistles. But we'd never talked much about how technology was moving and the opportunities that came with it. At our next meeting, I asked Doug to postpone the decision for two months so that we could start a weekly dialogue on leveraging technology, AI, and automation. He was reluctant at first. He believed that more features automatically meant better results and that I was being overly cautious. I persisted, promising that understanding how a particular software aligned with our needs would lead to better long-term decisions. That conversation made me realize my role was changing.

Because I understood the opportunities the right upgrade would bring, I needed Doug far more involved in tech-related decisions going forward. If the CEO isn't aware of opportunities brought on by a new system, it could compromise the company's ability to evaluate risk, understand growth, and stay on track. It's not that Doug needed to learn the details of UCaaS and CCaaS or every technical feature. But we had to address whether the technology enabled the growth and improvements we sought as a company. I helped Doug understand how different products affected how we could optimize client experiences or enhance communication between our headquarters and retail outlets.

I knew that stepping up to educate the board on the potential of technology decisions involved more from me on the business side. It also meant helping bridge gaps between departments. All that made me painfully aware of my own skill gaps. While strategizing was my strong suit, I wasn't known for my people skills speaking in plain business terms. I was the gatekeeper of cables and copper. I was comfortable with that image most of the time.

Doug and I started our weekly tech sessions, with partial results. I would drift off in IT talk, and Doug was impatient for me to get to the point. But as I found my footing in bringing him closer to the world of technology, he grew more interested, invited other department leaders to join us, and asked to extend our meetings for another month.

The more I succeeded in bringing my subject matter to others, the more it inspired me to consider what made leaders and influencers great. Above all, I started enjoying fostering connections and partnering with others both in and outside of the company. This experience has enabled me to step into my courage: the courage to stand firm in what I knew. AI and automation are the future, IT can drive real change in an organization, and I could lead this charge. As I faced Doug and let go of my protective bubble, I was able to solicit the support of others. Nothing can ever grow in isolation.

As for the company, at the end of what became our very first round of informal tech classes, we found a suitable cloud provider with solutions that fully aligned with our long-term goals. Consequently, we reduced costs and maintenance burden while streamlining our telecom services. We now have a customer-centric network that allows us to provide consistent client experiences, which has improved our brand's position. And with a solution partner that understands the importance of AI and automation, we're future-proof!

But more important than any specific results, we found our way as a team with the IT department in a central role. We saw firsthand what we can achieve when we empower technology to maximize the business side. As uncomfortable as it started, bringing everyone together was the best decision I ever made.

Owning Your Outcomes

During my time as a sales engineer, I observed company after company worrying more about processes than outcomes. They'd get some idea about how a particular system behavior should go and would lose sight of the reason they wanted it in the first place.

It's kind of like the time I read an article about how broccoli consumption was tied to better health outcomes. I went on a month-long broccoli-every-day kick. I was so focused on the what — eating broccoli — that I forgot about the why — better health outcomes. As it turns out, I already had control of all the health markers broccoli was supposed to improve — like lowering cholesterol. Forcing myself to eat broccoli every day only made me gassier, not healthier.

Save your team from the unpleasantness of over-rotating on a process by helping them measuring the outcome. For it's the outcomes that we want to boast about over dinner anyway.

IT's Measure of a Successful Project

When I asked some of my favorite IT folks who have experience doing contact center deployments how they define a successful project, I received a common response: "No complaints from agents!"

The tactical specificity of the remark made me chuckle. After all the effort IT puts in to ensure the integrations work, data flows smoothly, and the telecom aspects of the project cut over without incident, the one measure of success was: "No complaints from agents."

It made me realize how much subjective measures of success matter. Yes, please also define success by objective measures regarding functionality, stability, integrations, etc. But make sure you cover your reputational rear ends by considering the common IT-influenced gotchas that generate agent and supervisor complaints, such as:

- Can agents log in successfully?
- Do agents need to update/install software (browser, VDI, operating system, etc.)?
  - Were agents assigned the necessary permissions?
- Was any new software pre-installed?
- How is the call quality?
- Where can agents find training documents?
- Are the new processes documented?
- Are calls being recorded as expected?
  - Are the agent's desktop screens?
  - Where can you locate uploaded recordings?
- Do the new headsets work?

I think you get the idea. Agents or supervisors will perceive anything that slows them down as a planning or IT failure, even when it's an EBUAK[40]. Save yourself the hassle of defending your reputation by preserving it, defensively.

---

[40] Error between user and keyboard

Include one success criteria that demonstrates successful execution as a function of its impact on IT's workload — like the number of tickets opened during the first 15 days compared to the last rollout of a similarly transformational business application. Doing so will help you celebrate all the excellent planning your team performed. And it demonstrates to your leadership that a movement to the cloud is something you can expertly manage and something that will streamline business operations as a whole.

How Business Units Define a Successful Project

Depending on their place in the leadership hierarchy, your business unit partners will define success based on the results they see in their own space:

- Did we reduce handle times?
- Has customer satisfaction (CSAT) increased?
- How much does my contact center cost to operate per year?
- How did the IVA containment change?

Yet the challenge for many when it comes time to declare victory is they neglected to establish a baseline off which to compare the new solution. It's entirely possible (and even probable, in my experience) that the existing solution lacks the crucial reporting or source data necessary to document a baseline. And that might be a key motivation for the change in the first place. But it doesn't mean you shouldn't try.

To help business units own the outcome and celebrate great change, see what IT can do — as a final favor — with the old system. Can you access a data dump? Are there one-time analytics you can perform against which they can determine a baseline? If so, it's well worth the time. Not only will your team pocket political capital as the resident expert, but their success also becomes your success.

Reporting vs. Analytics and Insights

Reporting is knowing how much we weigh on a given day.

Analysis is evaluating that data and learning that we gain two pounds every year around our birthday — and never seem to lose it.

Insights occur when we realize that the one year our mom didn't bake us a cake was the one year our weight held steady.

Bad news for birthday cakes, but a helpful — if not depressing — insight for those trying to maintain a steady weight as they age.

IT should help the business appreciate the difference between reporting, analytics, and insights. Also remember these functions aren't necessarily performed by the same tool.

Our example included a bathroom scale, a spreadsheet, and the intelligence to integrate external data (Mom's baking hiatus). We wouldn't expect the bathroom scale to know what Mom was up to in 2019, so why would we expect a single reporting interface to provide all our insights? Sometimes we just need to know our weight. When we're ready to act on insights, we'll seek them.

Surprisingly few companies are ready to act. Only 16% of companies use insights to guide innovation, according to Walker's 2020 customer progress report[41]. Utilizing AI that can reach deep into your data and extract insights and, more importantly, apply those insights to your contact center practice can really set you apart from the competition.

Metrics to Consider

Multidimensional metrics move the needle further than any single metric ever can. Taken in concert, metrics track toward business outcomes. Individually, metrics can lead to overdoing it in one area.

Take a contact center that focuses sharply on occupancy rates — the percentage of time an agent is occupied or actively working

---

[41] *"Customers 2020: A Progress Report,"* Walker, https://walkerinfo.com/cxleader/customers-2020-a-progress-report/

on an interaction. One might naïvely assume a goal of 100% occupancy, but wise leaders know that agent stress rises steeply above a certain threshold. And customer satisfaction will subsequently tank when that happens. It's important to track one metric (CSAT) in context of the other (agent occupancy). No metric is an island.

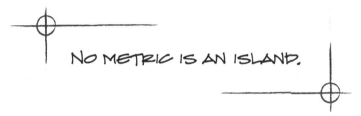

NO METRIC IS AN ISLAND.

Insights emerge when you consider why data trended in a particular direction, going beyond simply observing that a trend exists. The same goes with survey results. You need to be willing to ask your customers — or yourself — why they responded the way they did. Understanding the why lets you adapt and improve. Yet, only about one quarter of contact centers actually act on the results of their data analysis, according a 2022 survey by Metrigy.

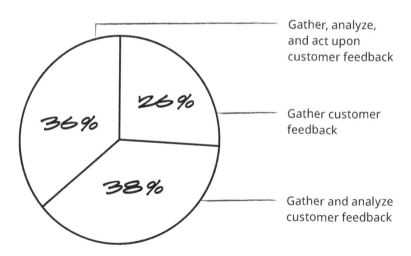

Figure 12-1: Approaches to customer feedback from "The Metrics Gap" by Robin Gareiss, Metrigy, 2022.

In short, staying competitive requires your contact center teams to treat yesterday's metrics as leading indicators, not final outcomes. Measure the outcome's metrics as a function of changes in the leading indicators. And remember you sometimes need intermediary metrics to bridge the gap.

For example, time spent on after-call work can impact your IVA's containment rate. How? Assuming no AI or automation joins the party, the less time agents spend taking notes, the less complete the notes become. This can impact downstream data flow and customer categorization. Subsequently, a customer might not be properly categorized or provided with the correct information during the IVA experience, which will impact containment. The problem is more likely to occur when a contact center supervisor tries to "optimize" after-call work time, thereby evaluating it in isolation.

Instead of encouraging the team to work faster — now understanding the impact of weak data on other KPIs — the supervisor should consider how technology can help. Offloading the time-consuming elements of after-call work to an AI tool can help them achieve the desired results without impacting the outcome: complete, actionable customer history.

And Metrics to Reconsider

Contact centers have used the same, stale metrics for years. Handed down from generation to generation of contact center leaders, these metrics live on like a fruitcake, way past their useful shelf life. In the spirit of advising your business peers — and perhaps for the Schadenfreude-fueled joy of blowing their minds a little — suggest tossing the following classic contact center metrics out a window.

Mean Time to Resolution (MTR)

So many factors go into the time it takes to resolve an issue, which, by the way, isn't the same as closing a case. An MTR metric is only useful if your contact center exclusively handles a very narrow selection of call types, like scheduling appointments. As you evolve your automation game and offload the very robotic functions of the call center onto self-service or AI-powered bots, your human agents will enjoy a more varied and more complex set of inquiries. These requests will naturally take a longer, less predictable amount of time. So, prepare to ditch the old way of measuring success.

Average Handle Time

For similar reasons to those with MTR, average handle time is becoming less and less meaningful. The way to salvage this familiar metric would be to evaluate it as a function of other data. What is the average handle time of interactions dispositioned[42] in a particular way? Or how did the handle time of interactions without a customer callback compare to those where the customer reached out a second time?

STALE METRICS LIVE ON LIKE A FRUITCAKE, WAY PAST THEIR USEFUL SHELF LIFE

---

[42] Disposition is a term used to describe an outcome. It's typically a reporting tag you put on the interaction. Most contact centers use dispositions to designate required follow-on actions, but some utilize them to describe the reason for the call.

PROCESS PIONEERS

Gerald Reports a Win

Gerald is a sales manager at a large education software retailer. His team covers several US and Canadian territories but was struggling to measure success as the company continued to grow. His experience as a teacher gave him a lot of tools to elevate his department and transform the way it handles quality control.

Gerald: I love telling the story about how I transformed my department at work. It is such a great example of making sure that you, as a company, know how to measure success. As a former teacher, I know better than anyone that measuring success properly is key when trying to see the bigger picture. Whether in the classroom or in a business, many companies haven't lined up the proper metrics to actually see employee performance. They only count costs and CSAT. Two-variable measurements does not a well-rounded hypothesis test make. This would be like grading students on their entire year based on one mid-year test!

When I began at my company, I was a burned-out teacher trying to take my skills into a different industry. I began by working in sales and oversaw smaller accounts until I worked my way up to a manager position. Loving the company and its mission, I always volunteered to take on new projects and dive into problem areas to see where we could improve. Upon my promotion to manager, I realized that we had a huge quality management issue. Our numbers were consistently below the goal markers our directors had set, and incremental changes weren't showing any impact.

One day, I was getting lunch with one of the IT supervisors who suggested that it wasn't that our numbers were wrong, the issue was with our chosen metrics. We had no way of capturing customer calls or chats for monitoring and evaluation. All our data was based on customer reviews and follow-up surveys. No one will put the effort into completing a survey unless they're upset about something.

We had yet to explore our entire CCaaS suite of features. It took some convincing to get my sales teams on board. They were originally worried about too much oversight and having that lead to company morale problems. I explained that, as it stood, employees who were thriving weren't being recognized and we had no way to properly maintain any sort of quality control. If you are killing it at your job day after day, wouldn't you want your bosses to know?

After much back and forth, we worked with IT to integrate quality management functionality into our workflow. Things changed in just about a week. Now we could easily listen to recorded calls and supervisors actually had something to use to coach their sales reps. The recording and screen share have also had major impact on the customer experience and have simplified coaching and feedback for agents. We've found that making agents feel supported during onboarding is the number one way to prevent turnover.

By switching our perspective, and our metrics, we were able to finally achieve our larger goal — to help the world learn.

CHAPTER THIRTEEN

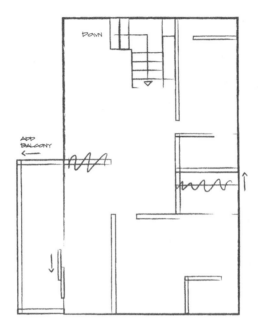

REMODELING

When my husband and I were shopping for a new place, we were astonished by how many "time capsule" apartments we saw. If the building was built in the 1970s, we could expect at least one unit that still had the original kitchen and bath finishes, and several with décor that screamed 1992. It's amazing how people get used to something and don't see anything out of place about putting a brand-new stainless-steel fridge into an otherwise disco-era kitchen.

As somebody who's experimenting with the notion of minimalism, I get it: Don't fix what ain't broken. In your personal life, that is an excellent way to cut spending and (hopefully) amass wealth. But in business, if you're not growing, you're contracting. If you're not changing, you're not improving. If you're not improving, you'll be surpassed by the competition — be it an eager 20-something with big ideas coming for your job, or an up-and-coming company gnawing at your market share. Competition is everywhere.

So, don't let your contact center forever home become a time capsule. Embrace and plan for the fact that you will remodel from time to time. Encourage ideas from the business users. Leverage your vendor's account team — like your technical account manager — and ask how you can apply new product features to improve your outcomes.

Business User Ownership

Remodels don't have to be difficult. Anyone who's watched HGTV knows a can of paint, roll of tape, and a little patience can elevate the experience of a formerly drab room.

Luckily, you've selected a cloud solution dedicated to making tools that make it easy for your business partners to help themselves. Encourage them to self-administer as much of the application as they are willing to take on.

Schedule "remodeling support" meetings at least two or three times a year. Use these as an opportunity to offer a fresh set of eyes and dust off your consulting hat. Together the teams will deliver results that evolve with changing market and customer expectations.

Developer Support

Since most contact centers don't have developer expertise on staff, it's likely your IT organization will continue to handle the development of any custom coding not outsourced to the vendor. While I'm sure it's part of your standard practices, consider this a friendly reminder that comments are your friend. People will come and go, but code commenting lasts forever. When you perform one-off customizations for — what I'm sure feels like —

a billion different business applications, it's tempting to just "get it done" and move on. But for the sake of your future remodeling selves: Stop, think, and annotate.

PEOPLE WILL COME AND GO, BUT CODE COMMENTING LASTS FOREVER.

Technical Debt Management

The team will inevitably make compromises during implementation. These less-than-ideal design choices become the seeds of technical debt. But if you acknowledge them during the design phase and document the reasons for the choices — detail the feature or existing functional behavior necessitating the selection — you'll be more likely to massage the implementation over time.

For example, if a missing API causes you to skip automating a data dip, forcing you to use a nightly batch-update process instead, document the requirements in a "binder of (remodeling) ambitions." I bet the vendor's sales team is aware of the missing feature and has likely entered it as a feature request. If it's in your binder, bring it up in your biannual (or, better, quarterly) meetings with the account team so you're made aware the moment the improved functionality becomes available.

The delivery of the feature request might not look like you originally imagined. At this point, however, your people are professional outcome spotters, and they'll appreciate and welcome the new method of doing things. Plus, it's probably better than what you envisioned in the first place — the feature got ran through a diverse customer feedback process, after all. It's important to focus on acknowledging when you plant a seed of technical debt, noting it, and watching for opportunities to "pull the weeds" with a mini remodel.

Predictions for the Future

While I sprinkled some food-for-thought leadership ideas along the way, my point in writing this book has been to share a pragmatic approach to contact center work. Next up, I'd like to focus on features and functionality I believe will become commonplace by 2030. (If anyone's reading this in 2030, drop me a line on LinkedIn — assuming that's still around — to tell me how I did!)

If we assume I'm at least partially on to something, you'd best select a solution provider that has already started designing and building in these directions. It's a long trek between ideas and commonplace adoption — and the trains are already leaving the station.

Omnichannel Becomes Uni-Channel

We spend a lot of time worrying about creating seamless customer experiences across channels. It's a noble goal that I highly recommend pursuing, but it feels like a Band-Aid. There will always be a new channel. My team formed a betting pool over the day that a request for a TikTok integration first crosses our desks. But continuously trying to sew separate threads into a single, historical ball of yarn only makes us a roadside spectacle — not a thought leader.

Instead, I imagine a world where there is only one thread: your conversation with the customer. In this future we've mastered the art of customer identification and can hook all communication modalities onto the single thread. I message you on chat for a couple minutes, then switch to SMS because I switched devices, then start a video meeting because I'm walking and don't feel like typing. Eventually I move to voice when I lose my Wi-Fi signal.

If the interaction were all represented by a single "Erin" thread inside the contact center that paused and resumed as I dis- and re-engaged, it would allow me to interact with the business as naturally as I do with my friends. It would also necessitate that the industry refresh how it thinks about interactions as something other than finite events with clear conclusions (dispositions). Instead realizing that your customer relationships are as fluid as ice cubes in Miami — they will flow where they flow. When we stop trying to connect and relate a bunch of discrete interactions, we'll be free to rethink how we route, how we service, and how we engage our customers. That'd be nice.

Truly Conversational AI

What we call conversational AI today is cool, but it's a façade — if we're being honest. Sure, we can use natural language processing to ascertain customer intent, but we still have to write, script, and code the responses. Somebody on the team needs to go in, train the AI, map customer utterances to programmed intents, and craft clever comebacks. It seems conversational and very engaging to the customer. But to the programmer, it's labor intensive. In fact, I'd argue that the reason you don't encounter more conversational bots today has nothing to do with the technology. It exists. The issue is that the people writing the code either aren't creative enough to script conversational dialogs or they don't have the time and budget to complete the complex process it requires.

I don't see us achieving conversational AI until the AI can write its own responses. We've seen it, sort of, when IBM's Watson played *Jeopardy!*. But I've also seen it in the technology emerging from organizations like Open.ai. As we get closer to living alongside AI that can generate responses that pass the Turing test, I imagine it will make a huge impact on the contact center.

What if you could point one of these systems that "knows" the internet at your business's catalog of knowledge? Instead of your team defining a book of intents and mapping them to your FAQ responses, the AI would take care of it. It would know your business as well as a human agent, could search all your documentation for solutions, and then combine what it finds with the "common sense" information on the internet.

I imagine use cases like this:

> **Me:** I need a new pair of sneakers.
> **Bot:** I think these would look great on you. <Sends pictures>

Boom! The entire middle of a typical bot-led conversation is missing. How is this possible? What happened on the back end? Well, the bot understood sneakers to mean shoes of a certain category. Maybe it consulted the business's product catalog and narrowed the selection to ladies' athletic shoes. Then it surmised that the weather near my South Florida residence would suggest I'd prefer sneaks with good airflow. Perhaps it consulted my Instagram to determine that I love colorful clothing and reviewed my retail history to sort out my size. At some point, all by itself, the bot reduced the number of options in the catalog to a pair that lined up with all its data. The point is the bot actually embraced the spirit of my intent, at least as well as the average human salesman, without involving me directly with its selection process. I didn't need to answer a bunch of fixed questions about fit, price, or preference because there was enough information out there to sort it out on its own.

Now could you do that today? Technically yes, with a boatload of programming. But I'd prefer to imagine the future where the AI actually "works out" the problem on its own and our teams don't have to tell it when or where to look for data, how to apply it, or consider every conversational permutation.

Effortless After-Call Work

In the same way true conversational AI would revolutionize self-service, its integration inside the contact center could take the work out of after-call work. An AI that understood conversations would listen to the customer and agent's discussion, apply what it knows from its experience (your company's library, the internet, etc.), and generate not only call summaries, but the reason for the call. We'd no longer be tied to singular dispositions and their resulting singular workflows. The AI, like a concierge, would initiate all post-interaction business processes, own the memorialization — a thoughtful summary, and even provide observations about the call to the agent.

Imagine that: The time agents currently spend on typing notes could be spent on an immediate debrief on the call. The AI can act as a supervisor, providing tips about tone, pace, and content — suggesting better ways for the agent to approach the problem in the future — and even recommend a quick training class. By providing quality feedback at the end of every call, you ensure that the team will do better next time, every time. Plus, since this is probably the same AI powering your IVA, every call it listens to improves its ability to help customers self-serve. Now that's what I'm talking about.

Independent Administration

All this AI doesn't mean the system will administer itself. At least I don't expect that to become common within the next few years, but I do expect the administration — especially the collaborative intelligence and AI components — to become drop-dead intuitive.

Today several companies are diligently delivering tools to democratize the administration of their platforms to put power in the hands of the people using it. We've already (mostly) said goodbye to language scientist requirements for natural language. In the next few years, to stand a chance at achieving my other predictions as an industry, contact center providers must continue to step up the administrative game.

Agents should be able to visualize a customer's entire experience, the whole journey, on a single experiential thread. We should easily discover opportunities for improvement. Implementing changes should take little time. Error detection and testing should be baked into the design process and occur automatically with every save.

In the future, I see administrators needing only to know their business, not to also become experts on the platform.

PROCESS PIONEERS

Bob: A BPO Remodel Master

Bob works in IT at a BPO. His company's biggest client is a frozen foods delivery service that contracts his firm to help with customer complaints during the busy holiday seasons. Bob is used to time-sensitive requests from his clients and, given the recent economic uncertainty, has begun to consider how he can help preserve margins and differentiate his BPO among the competition.

Bob: I knew the stakes couldn't be higher this holiday season. Our biggest client is in the frozen foods business. If you can serve it for dinner during the holidays, they're ready to ship it. Unfortunately, they were hit with some unpleasant realities in the first holiday season following the pandemic.

To put it lightly, all their costs had gone up, from raw ingredients to packaging materials and the fuel to ship to customer doorsteps. Supply-chain issues made margins suddenly razor thin. Complicating this was the fact that theirs is a largely seasonal business. The vast majority of the company's annual revenue comes in the form of products ordered in November and December.

Any issues during these months could be catastrophic and jeopardize the business as a whole. Given that they're our biggest client, it would be devastating for us as well. Their shrinking margins combined with our rising labor costs put increased pressure on our contract. We were dangerously close to not turning a profit. We couldn't lose them.

Their first customer service issues started pouring in just after Halloween. Everybody wanted to know the same thing: Why am I paying more today than I did a year ago? I don't blame people for asking.

I started thinking about how we could use technology to communicate answers quickly, efficiently, and respectfully. We needed our agents to make the customers feel heard and valued, just as if they had called the company directly. Our top priority is always to treat our customers' customers like our own.

Unfortunately, our system for handling customer calls had been relatively stagnant since I started here. If you opened a chat window or picked up a phone, you'd wind up talking to a live agent who would do their best to resolve your issue. We were what the industry calls a true "butts in seats" BPO. This provides a human touch, but it's also problematic. Humans can only do so much. And they're expensive to hire. If a lot of customers had an issue all at once, they'd wind up stuck on hold. The only thing worse is an angry customer who is also hungry. Hangry customers: That's generally who call us.

Customers complaining about prices was only the beginning. Supply issues caused my daughter's Halloween costume to show up in November. My favorite hot sauce hadn't been in stock at the grocery store for two months. The world had been impacted over the last year and shockwaves reverberated through every purchase. We had become so used to anything we wanted arriving right away that it was jarring when it didn't happen. Add in that it was happening during the already stressful holiday season and prices were higher: We had to get ahead of this.

I knew that it would take more than adding staff to answer calls. Our client couldn't afford the expense, and we had overseas competitors who could offer the same thing at a fraction of the cost. I also had to figure out a way to make sure we were handling call volume while still addressing the standard phone orders. If we slipped on either of those categories, it would hurt our client's already narrow margins and might send them packing.

I sat down with my department head and said we need a way to automate answers to common questions. Given the repetitive and predictable questions we fielded for nearly all our clients, I jokingly suggested we should build a robot that answered all the repetitive requests. We'd recapture some of our margins and help our clients scale. Neither of us took the idea seriously until lunch later in the week.

My wife made her signature lasagna using plant-based meat for dinner the night before and I had packed leftovers for lunch. A coworker could smell me heating it in the microwave and remarked how good it smelled. "Honestly, I can't tell the difference between this and the real thing sometimes," I replied. Then the lightbulb went on.

If we could build a bot that customers didn't recognize as a bot, one that felt like they were talking to a person, we could offload some of the call volume. If we can make fake meat taste like real meat, surely we can design a human-enough bot to engage with customers. In that moment I decided that instead of adding staff, I'd build some bots and put them on the job.

We'd use automated chat, voice, and intelligent virtual agents. We'd immediately send any callers looking to place an order to a human to handle the lucrative upsell script. But we'd redirect any complaints to the virtual agent that would help them understand the price hikes and delays.

The crucial component to all of this was the cost of one virtual agent was essentially 10% of the cost of hiring a person. We'd be able to pass massive savings directly on to our client, who could turn around and pass them on to customers in the form of lowered costs and loyalty coupons. I pitched this solution to our client relations director, who instantly agreed this was the right course of action.

Sure enough, supply-chain issues caused issues across industries that holiday season. We were ready. Our virtual agents were standing by to track packages, provide information, and help keep customers happy. The customer satisfaction surveys at the end of the holiday season were the highest they've ever been: Customers felt like their business was valued and their dollar was stretched as far as it could go in these trying times.

Business has been forever changed as a result of that holiday season. The virtual agents are the gift that keeps on giving.

CHAPTER FOURTEEN

HAPPILY EVER AFTER

Maybe 14 months after we moved into the condo, I realized I was home. Until this point I loved the place, but having moved so many times over the years, I still thought of it as a temporary stop on the way to our next adventure. To the point where my husband and I even discussed (hypothetically) selling it all when we retire and being nomads for a few years, following the siren song of the world — wherever it called us.

Something changed around the 14-month mark — and no, it wasn't interest rates — that made us realize we were home. I'm not sure if it was the realization that the layout is truly unique, my love affair with beach life, or our new minimalist approach to design and living. The place just feels like us, like home.

Hopefully by now you're feeling the work equivalent. With nothing left to do you can let out your breath, ease into the recliner, and just be. It's finally time for you to assume your new role in the contact center of the future.

Strategic Decision Maker

If you followed my advice thus far, you've already made great strides to modernize the perception of IT's role in the contact center. You've stepped away from the closet of copper cabling and into the role of trusted advisor. Having proven yourself, maintain your momentum: Step into the role of strategic decision maker.

This might seem like a leap, but you've laid all the groundwork. You've amassed a great deal of industry knowledge. You've explored and evaluated cutting-edge contact center technology platforms. You're the resident expert on AI and automation. You advised the contact center team on how to become more efficient, more effective, and more engaging. And, most important, you've built bridges between the contact center and the rest of the organization, a feat long overdue.

Who knows how the data, analytics, and insights flow between departments better than you? Who provided actionable insights to marketing? Helped sales speak to more customers, more effectively? All while revising and streamlining their own help-desk practices? You did, buddy. You did!

Share the wins with your leadership team, focusing primarily on the outcomes. Before long they will come to you and your IT team for strategic advice because that's where it lives now.

Effects on the Team

As your role evolved, so did the roles on your team. My advice on how to cascade this newfound responsibility depends largely on the structure of your organization. For the sake of simplicity, assume you either mostly align your team behind supporting products and solutions or departments.

AI Master

Those on "camp product" will want to consider adding a specialty role for management of AI solutions. While individual contact center leaders will have the requisite skills to train existing AI agents, they may not fully grasp enough AI philosophy to thrive with the responsibility of designing new AI agents and models. A specialized, expert member of your team can dig deep into the spirit of the AI tools, both advising on and implementing solutions that maximize the AI investments.

IVA Designer

A subspeciality of AI is the IVAs that drive voice and chat bots. Again, a situation where the tool your vendor provides should be "clicks, not code" but where deep design expertise can help. IT professionals accustomed to programming different vectors for on-premises applications will appreciate this change to a visual editor while enjoying the ability to still contribute code snippets as needed to accomplish business unit goals.

Having a team member specializing on this solution segment will provide more opportunities to extend functionality beyond the contact center. Think: What's the experience when people call the company HQ? In my experience, dedicating an IT specialist in this area and training them to take a consultative point-of-view when gathering business requirements allows for more creative, engaging outcomes for customers — external and internal. It should also result in a better application of AI features than those designed and implemented within the business units.

Usability Specialist

I use the term usability to mean both customer and agent experiences. Typically, the marketing department will have someone on staff (or retainer) to help ensure the website meets ADA standards. But who looks out for the employees and customers of the contact center? Your team.

Investing the time to train a member of the IT team to understand usability will allow you to deliver value to the whole organization — once you establish your sea legs in the contact center, of course. To start, consider areas of usability including:

- Ergonomics of the agent workspace, like headset fit
- Languages your IVA understands and speaks
- Speed and frequency with which prompts repeat
- How much time you allow a customer to respond before re-prompting

It's more than simply complying with laws; this is about creating a pleasant experience for every user.

An Opportunity for Diversity and Inclusion

For many contact centers, this will be the first time they approach AI and automation, which means there is no in-house expertise. You might look around your organization and realize IT doesn't yet have the expertise either. That's okay. Expected even. I point it out because I think it's an opportunity for you to achieve some of the less-spoken corporate goals — specifically around diversity, equity, and inclusion (DE&I).

Since no one currently has the experience, there's no reason we can't choose to invest in a team of individuals that might more closely represent your company's DE&I goals. Look around. How many people of color are on your team? How many women? Women of color? Members of the LGBTQIA+ community? Single parents? Immigrants? First-generation college grads? Veterans? People who are differently abled? Now ask yourself: Is this also an opportunity to better represent the communities you serve?

Look, you have to train someone on the topic anyway, so take the opportunity, branch out, diversify.

Effective DE&I strategies acknowledge that access to the opportunity (for training) is often the first barrier minority groups face. Those already there, the people already "in the room" get first dibs on the training and growth opportunities.

So maybe reach down, or around, and see if you can't find a future, eager-to-learn AI and automation master somewhere in the org or community who also contributes expertise and the kind of fresh perspective your company needs as it embarks on this AI-powered transformation journey.

Cross the Streams, Get Better Outcomes

To teams on "camp business unit," I have a simple reminder from *Ghostbusters*: Cross the streams. Sure, the threaded message in *Ghostbusters* was to "never cross the streams," but if we recall, in the end, that's how they tackled the final villain. In business, when you cross the streams, you also get BIG outcomes.

A key theme throughout the book has been to measure, analyze, and share insights. IT can add continuous value by being the facilitator of that information and insight flow. Schedule regular meetings between different team members to share ideas. Even better, make it a part of your weekly stand-up. Have the person assigned to the contact center share an opportunity or idea for collaboration or simply report on a result that might interest one of their peer's departments. Over time the collaborative culture will catch on, so stick with it. Like in *Ghostbusters*, it's difficult at first, but it's the best way to bring down the big, bad guy — your business's BHAG[43].

PROCESS PIONEERS

Alisha Redefines Her Role

Alisha has been working since 2019 for an accredited public health department with more than 1,000 employees. In 2017, she moved from CTO to CIO. Despite her love for

---

[43] Big, hairy, audacious goal

her job, it took a steep learning curve for Alisha to realize how she could better support her organization in reimagining the patient and public experience through its multiple contact centers.

Alisha: *COVID-19.* Is there anyone out there who doesn't get an emotional reaction to these words? When the pandemic first hit, it almost cost me my job and sanity. It ripped our collective inadequacies open and made everyone face hard realizations. But every challenge also bears a seed of opportunity. What I learned about myself when I confronted my weaknesses changed my life and career for the better.

I used to believe that we couldn't afford to modernize all our software at once. For one thing, I work for a government entity, so we're always looking for ways to stretch taxpayer dollars. For another, our legacy system was performing well over the years, even if it gradually began draining our resources. We had limited ability to scale call volumes, but I took pride in the way my team found creative workarounds.

I knew we would eventually have to make a full move to the cloud. But I also wanted to be smart about it, so I created a five-year digital transformation strategy that I considered bulletproof. The goal was to work our way through our priority list progressively. For example, to address employee burnout, we would further utilize Microsoft Teams integrations so our agents could start working remotely.

In hindsight, I didn't fully appreciate how much the old system hindered our growth because my ability to maintain it proved I knew what I was doing. Our customers received stable and consistent service, so I was convinced that my cost-saving solution — which didn't require a lift-and-shift approach — made perfect sense.

Oh boy, was I wrong.

We were in the beginning stages of digital transformation when COVID-19 hit. Overnight, life and work as we knew them changed. There was a flood of calls we couldn't handle: We went from 50 a day to more than 700! Worse yet, we had to send our staff home without a setup that allowed them to work remotely.

My "aha" moment didn't take long. I realized that my reluctance to choose appropriate tech solutions for our business goals informed my company's inability to pivot.

I was almost in a frozen state on the day I had a talk with my boss Steve, our CFO. Steve was kind and supportive, but I felt guilty that his proactive search for a solution felt like indirect blame. The next day, although my first impulse was to hide away, I had another talk with Steve and our CEO, which helped me out of the self-blame mode. We had to do a lot of damage control in minimal time — days, ideally hours, as even our executives were drowning in the flood of calls.

And we did it: We found the right software and migrated to the cloud in just 48 hours, with an easy transition I would have never thought possible had I not witnessed it firsthand.

The situation with COVID-19 had highlighted the inefficiencies in our system and approach, but it also made me aware of my shortcomings as a leader. Even before the pandemic, remote care and contactless patient/staff interactions were on the rise. Had we replaced our old software sooner, we would have had more flexibility and room for expanding and streamlining workflows.

I've since become a better strategist and learned to consider trends and the long-term implications of everyday decisions. I'm also much more curious about how we can utilize collaborative intelligence: The future belongs to those who combine human approaches with automation.

Fast-forward two years: I am in a very different place than at the start of the pandemic. I'm more confident and enjoy contributing to both tactical and strategic conversations with other leaders. Letting go of my command-and-control thinking took time, but it all fell into place as I began seeing innovation and first-principles thinking as a better way to structure our people, processes, and technology. I now know that there's more to it than an obsessive cost-effective approach and have tasked my colleagues with letting me know if I ever get wrapped up in a pet project that carries me away from the big picture.

But the biggest lesson has been the importance of stepping out of my comfort zone. I am grateful to my executive team for allowing me the space to grow. And I'm committed to empowering my team in the same way.

CONCLUSION

As I neared the end of writing this book, I came across an interview with Matt Dixon on Douglas Burdett's The Marketing Book Podcast. The author of several successful books including *The Challenger Sale*[44], Dixon was promoting his latest: *The JOLT Effect*[45]. Their conversation introduced the idea that — despite what many sales representatives have been taught — most of the deals they lost to "no decision" weren't lost because they hadn't established sufficient FOMO[46]. Instead, the prospect had an unresolved fear of messing up (FOMU). Dixon suggests that FOMU makes us decision-adverse for three reasons:

- We have too many choices and don't want to pick the wrong one.
- We don't feel like we know enough to expertly decide.
- There's no guarantee we'll achieve the outcomes we've been promised.

---

[44] *The Challenger Sale: Taking Control of the Customer Conversation*, Matthew Dixon and Brent Adamson, Portfolio 2011.

[45] *The JOLT Effect: How High Performers Overcome Customer Indecision*, Matthew Dixon and Ted McKenna, Portfolio, 2022.

[46] Fear of missing out

After meticulously detailing all the aspects of a seasoned, reasoned contact center decision, you can imagine my horror when I realized I may have given you too much information. Have I inadvertently set you up to fall victim to the paradox of choice[47]? I hope not. And if I have, I'm sorry. Just in case, here's some final advice before I send you off to the races.

Lean on the Sales Team

I'm not inclined to voluntarily relinquish control or show my vulnerable underbelly to people with whom I might later have to negotiate. But I've learned that sharing feelings of indecision — even indirectly — can help you move past the analysis paralysis. Like asking a server in a restaurant for an entrée recommendation, it's completely fair to ask your sales team for input when selecting configurations, packages, or options.

And remember, by choosing a cloud solution, you're not locked into any specifics. Flexible contracting terms, dynamic feature sets, and SLAs will help you mitigate risk-related, FOMU anxiety. Plus, we're all human. If we mess up, we learn and move on. That's the promise of the cloud, after all: It allows you to adapt to changing market conditions. (Maybe one of those changing conditions is your level of wisdom.)

4 Things You Can Do Today

By now I trust I've inspired you to make some changes and construct the contact center of the future inside your company. You know it's time and will make a change — just as soon as you follow the steps in this book (and secure funding). But let's not let corporate mechanics get in the way of inspired action. Here are four things you can do today to add value inside your contact center.

---

[47] *The Paradox of Choice: Why More Is Less,* Barry Schwartz, Ecco, 2004.

One: Make Introductions

Strategic networking is the first step to positioning yourself as an expert advisor inside your company. So, start connecting with contact center and marketing leadership in a casual way. Get to know them and start gradually sharing your insights. Then, introduce the marketing leaders to the contact center leaders. As we've learned, there is a lot of overlapping value that contact center data can bring to marketing. Once both sides understand the value they can provide each other and the business, they'll surely support your quest to build them a castle in the sky.

Two: Find a Vendor That Matches Your Vibe

Even if you're not ready to roll out the blueprints just yet, it's still a good time browse vendors. Go to a trade show, fill out a few online forms, have lunch with a few vendor reps. You're about to embark on a digital transformation that will require partnership and trust, neither of which is built overnight. Use the calm before the storm to find a vendor or two with whom you jive. Not only will they help provide the educational support you need early on, you'll save yourself the headache of dealing with salespeople you don't like once the real work begins.

Three: Share This Book

There are a lot of side roads along the way to your contact center dream home. Walking into a boardroom with as many ideas as I've shared in this book will likely overwhelm the decision committee. You don't want to overcomplicate the initial conversations. Help your peers gain the perspective you now enjoy as you lead up to the buying exercise. Creating a shared vantage point will surely help all those involved to trust in the wisdom IT will bring to the process. And it may even inspire them to — dare I say — ask for your help.

Four: Dip Your Toe

If your organization isn't yet financially, or emotionally, prepared to move to the cloud, consider other ways you can move toward cloud-powered technologies. Intelligent virtual agents, for example, allow you to breathe some life into your on-premises infrastructure. By layering a modern solution onto your technology stack, you can demonstrate early results. And remember, these technologies may actually fund the rest of your digital transformation.

PROCESS PIONEERS

Justin: Bringing Teams Together

In the contact center of the future, IT is as much matchmaker as consultant. Adopting this new perspective allowed Justin, who works in marketing for a national pizza chain, to stand out. Justin's go-getter attitude was immediately attractive to his employers. Around four years ago, the company had deployed a cloud-based virtual agent solution to handle calls, which completely streamlined the way it does business. With a minor in computer science, Justin realized he could apply the contact center technology to work they were doing in marketing.

Justin: I've never been one to stand around and wait for someone to tell me what to do. Growing up with eight siblings, you had to jump in and get the job done or be left behind. Marketing always spoke to me as a career option because I love business. But more so, I love studying people and the trends that result from their behavior. After uni, I floated around a bit before landing at my current company. Immediately, I saw opportunity there. In many companies, higher-ups sequester marketing from everyone else.

While I understand accounting getting protective of its budgets, this style of business has never worked for me and fortunately, it never worked for my company. They promoted weekly Lunch and Learns where people from all over the company would get together and network. We discussed what we did, how we excelled at our job, and what could be better.

This is how I started to meet people from IT and customer service. Most people find that their workflow best works hand-in-hand with sales, so I'm not sure many people took the opportunity to really learn what IT does. I heard about a new CCaaS platform. My IT contacts seemed genuinely surprised that I wanted to hear more and get a tutorial.

When I finally got a software demo, I was stunned. Why were we hiding this? While designed to streamline calls and automate orders, there was a ton of on-demand reporting that aggregates customer interaction data and highlights trouble spots. While contact center supervisors used it to troubleshoot, I also wanted access. Where else could I access firsthand information about actual customer conversations so easily?!?

Part of me toyed with the idea of keeping this gold mine to myself. But in the end, I knew that if everyone in marketing had access to call volumes, reasons for abandoned orders, and such, we could build entire campaigns around it. Forecasting demand is a huge part of our work, but people don't realize where that data needs to come from.

For example, timing is everything in marketing. By shifting our TV spots by a mere 30 minutes, we avoided promoting ourselves during times when the contact center was already busy. Aligning with a low-interaction volume time meant we could allocate more staff to proactive chats, resulting in a 15% drop in abandoned orders on our website. Little adjustments can make a huge difference in a company this large.

But it was an uphill battle convincing the VPs in customer success to let marketing have the unfettered access we wanted. After months of campaigning, and with the help of my IT partner, they gave us a one-month trial period. It felt like that scene from Indiana Jones when Indy is finally reaching the golden idol. I swore I heard a hallelujah chorus coming from my computer that day.

My team had one shot. We ran an entire campaign around a certain holiday, offering digital coupons through an interactive game of sorts. Because we had asked for reporting around calls vs. online orders in the immediate follow-up, we could see that our advertising flooded online sales but left our phone orders relatively static. On the other hand, when we ran TV spots, we could know exactly where those calls came from and isolate the demographics of people influenced by those ads vs. our digital campaign. What's more, we could forecast that if our strategy moving forward was investing heavily in digital, we didn't need to scale our voice resources as much and could focus on IT and chat function support instead.

Now we understand how people are working. We're using data to see how orders are handled and whether our ad campaigns had the desired effect we want to invest in. I'm grateful that the IT department supported the cross pollination, allowing me to make a name for myself and help the company drive revenue. Win, win.

Let's Go!

There's an XKCD comic called "Bridge[48]" where the characters humorously play out the classic conversation:

Mom: You can't go!
Me: But everyone else...
Mom: If all your friends jumped off a bridge, would you jump too?

At this point the character deviates from the norm, responding with "Oh jeez, probably." Naturally, his mom is confused by the response, but he shares his logic: Was it more likely that all his friends — many levelheaded and afraid of heights — all went crazy, simultaneously? Or could it be that the bridge is on fire?

I love this notion and have since used it to describe the situation when you see a bunch of early employees start to leave once a company reaches a certain size of scale. For them, the bridge is on fire: The company culture is getting too "corporate" and it's time for all the "startup people" to jump to the next new, exciting project.

So, why is everyone flocking to the cloud? Have they all gone nuts? Or is the on-premises bridge on fire?

I think you know where I stand.

Make the leap. Keep the promise. Deliver results.

MAKE THE LEAP.
KEEP THE PROMISE.
DELIVER RESULTS.

---

[48] https://xkcd.com/1170/

ACKNOWLEDGEMENTS

This book would not have been possible without the support and encouragement of my Five9 family. Thank you to everyone who took the time to assist with my research, sanity checks, and ideation sessions. A special acknowledgement goes out to Kim Austin for her expert editing eye, and Arthur Waidhofer for the beautiful illustrations — they really brought the ideas to life. I'd also like to thank Merideth K., Dashiell D., Marijan H., Jelena P., and Felix W., who brought our customer characters to life. Finally, a thank you to Genefa Murphy for supporting this ambitious project — I hope it proved worth it.

Made in the USA
Monee, IL
06 March 2023